insight text guide

Fiona Gregory

The Importance of Being Earnest

Oscar Wilde

First published in 2009. Reprinted in 2012, 2016, 2021, 2022, 2023.

Insight Publications Pty Ltd
3/350 Charman Road
Cheltenham VIC 3192
Australia
Tel: +61 3 8571 4950
Fax: +61 3 8571 0257
Email: books@insightpublications.com.au

www.insightpublications.com.au

National Library of Australia Cataloguing-in-Publication entry:
Gregory, Fiona.
Oscar Wilde's The importance of being earnest : insight text guide / Fiona Gregory.
1st ed.
9781921411007 (pbk.)
Insight text guide.
Bibliography.
For secondary school age.
Wilde, Oscar, 1854–1900 Importance of being earnest.
822.89

Cover design: The Modern Art Production Group

Printed by Markono Print Media Pte Ltd

contents

CHARACTER MAP

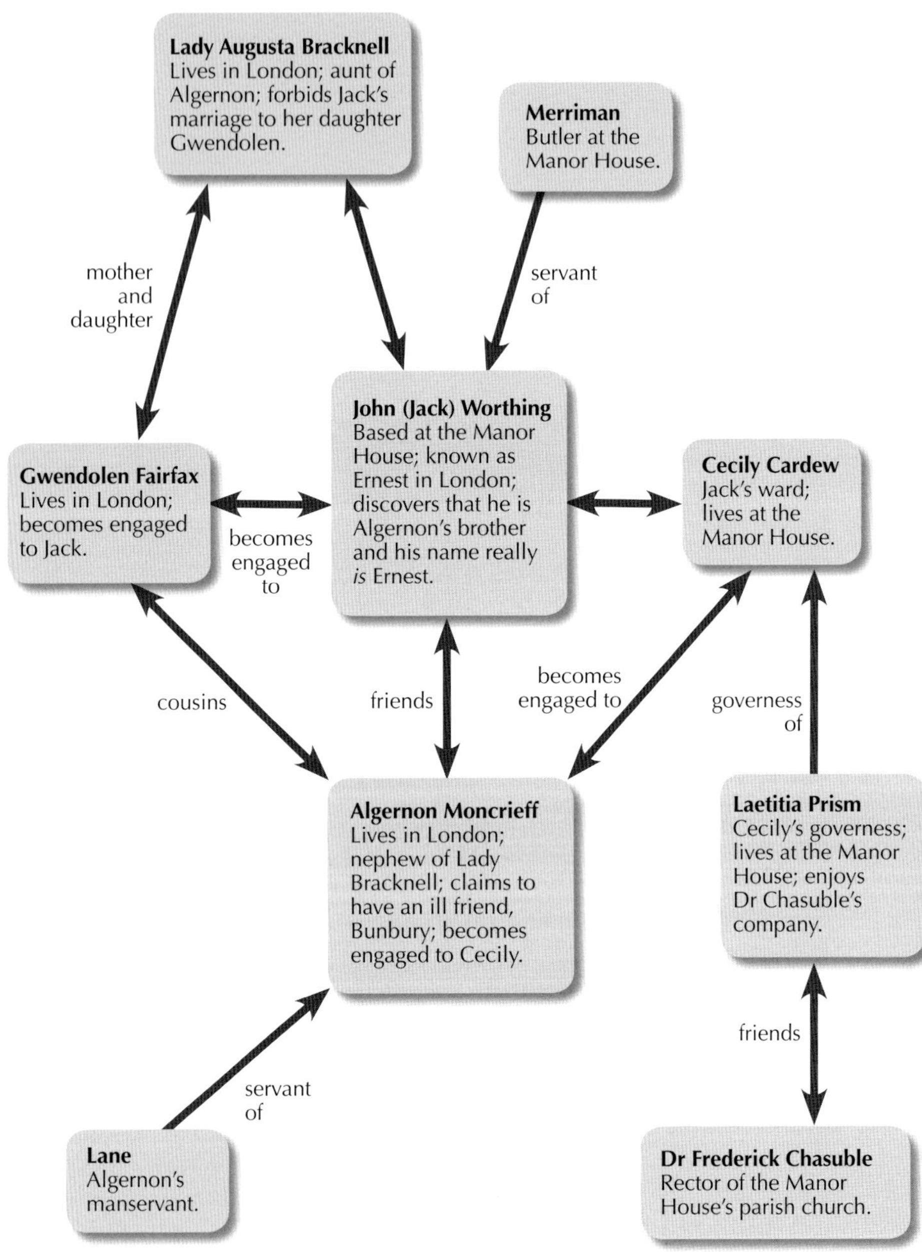

OVERVIEW

About the author

Oscar Fingal O'Flahertie Wills Wilde was born in Dublin, Ireland in 1854. His father was a successful surgeon and his mother was a committed Irish nationalist and writer. Wilde excelled at school and later studied Classics at Trinity College, Dublin and Magdalen College, Oxford. In 1878 Wilde moved to London, where he built a career in writing and editing. The forms of his writing ranged from essays and children's stories to the novel, poetry and drama; it is for the latter that he is best known today. In his own time, Wilde was renowned for his wit and outrageous fashion sense, and was recognised as a leading figure of Aestheticism, an artistic movement that called for the celebration of beauty as its own reward.

In the 1880s, Wilde was a celebrity in the modern sense – he was more famous than his works. His attitudes and opinions were frequently satirised in the popular media. In 1881, Gilbert and Sullivan's comic opera *Patience* parodied the Aesthetic movement and Wilde in particular. His becoming the subject of parody is an indication of Wilde's status at this time, as is the fact that he was invited to tour the United States in 1882 with a series of lectures on Aesthetics.

Wilde married Constance Lloyd in 1884 and they had two sons, Cyril (born in 1885) and Vyvyan (born in 1886), to whom their father was devoted. The fairytales he devised for the children were published as *The Happy Prince and Other Tales* in 1888. Wilde's first and only novel *The Picture of Dorian Gray* appeared in 1891. This was also the year Wilde met Lord Alfred Douglas, or 'Bosie' as he was known: Wilde's relationship with Bosie would lead to his downfall.

Before this, however, Wilde enjoyed a brilliant period of success between 1892 and 1895 when four of his plays (*Lady Windermere's Fan, A Woman of No Importance, An Ideal Husband* and *The Importance of Being Earnest*) achieved popular and critical acclaim on the London stage. In 1893, Wilde's daring play *Salome*, based on a biblical character, was refused a licence by the Lord Chamberlain's Office, which censored all plays appearing in London. *Salome* was finally staged by the great actress and theatre producer Sarah Bernhardt in Paris in 1896.

Despite the success he enjoyed in the early 1890s, Wilde was in danger. Bosie's father, the Marquess of Queensbury, was suspicious of the playwright's relationship with his son and determined to destroy Wilde. Two weeks after the opening of *The Importance of Being Earnest*, Wilde – who was now living apart from his wife – received the Marquess of Queensbury's card. Written on the card was: 'To Oscar Wilde, posing somdomite' (the word Queensbury meant here was 'sodomite'). Against the advice of his friends, Wilde brought a charge of libel against Queensbury. Wilde lost the case and, as homosexuality was a criminal offence, was subsequently arrested and charged with Gross Indecency under the Criminal Law Amendment Act. In May 1895, Wilde was found guilty and sentenced to two years' hard labour. The trials garnered enormous public interest and the popular press poured vitriol (severe criticism) on Wilde. As an Irishman who at times expressed radical political views and frequented the homosexual underworld, Wilde was essentially an 'outsider' and held a precarious position in Victorian England. The scorn and suspicion that had been kept in check during his years of success were fully unleashed following the trials.

Upon his release from prison in 1897, Wilde travelled to France. He was ill, impoverished and estranged from his family; Constance refused all contact and had changed her own and the boys' surname. Wilde continued to hope for reconciliation with his wife but she died in 1898. Wilde pursued a restless existence but continued to write; his long verse poem 'The Ballad of Reading Gaol' was published in 1898. Wilde finally settled in Paris, where he died on 30 November 1900.

Synopsis

Algernon Moncrieff is making preparations for a visit from his aunt Lady Bracknell and cousin Gwendolen when a friend calls. This friend, referred to by Algernon as 'Ernest', is in fact John – or Jack – Worthing.

Jack is pleased to hear of the impending arrival of Gwendolen as he has come to town to propose to her. Algernon objects when Jack informs him of this plan, as he has seen the affectionate message from a female named 'Cecily' inscribed in Jack's cigarette case. After some attempts to disguise Cecily's identity, Jack is forced to reveal that she is his ward, whose care was entrusted to him by her late grandfather. Upon this revelation a deeper secret emerges as Jack admits that his name is not actually Ernest. In order to escape the responsibilities of his country estate, Jack has developed a fictional younger brother, 'Ernest', who lives a life of pleasure in London. Algernon is delighted to hear Jack's story as he is also leading a double life, having created a fictional friend, Bunbury, who is frequently in need of his assistance out of town.

Lady Bracknell and Gwendolen arrive at the flat and Algernon manoeuvres his aunt out of the room so that Jack can propose to Gwendolen. Gwendolen readily accepts Jack's offer although she stresses that her love for him is dependent on the fact of his being named 'Ernest'. Jack resolves to have himself secretly re-christened. Lady Bracknell abruptly re-enters the room and ejects Gwendolen from the flat before subjecting Jack to a gruelling interview in which he is forced to reveal that he was discovered as a baby in a handbag in the cloakroom of Victoria Station. Lady Bracknell is horrified by Jack's story and refuses to allow his marriage to Gwendolen unless he can trace the identity of his parents. Following Lady Bracknell's departure, Gwendolen returns to reiterate her devotion to Jack and asks for his address in the country, which is overheard and noted by Algernon. Jack resolves to simplify his life by killing Ernest.

Act Two moves to Jack's country estate where Cecily is taking lessons with her governess Miss Prism. Having encouraged Miss Prism to take a walk in the garden with the local curate Dr Chasuble, Cecily is surprised by the arrival of Algernon posing as Jack's brother Ernest. Cecily reveals a lively interest in the misdeeds of Ernest, and the two exit the garden. Miss Prism and Dr Chasuble return from their walk to welcome the sudden arrival home of Jack, who announces the death of his brother Ernest. Amidst their condolences Jack arranges with Dr Chasuble to have himself re-christened. Cecily enters to announce the arrival of Ernest. In the presence of his household, Jack is forced to shake hands with Algernon and publicly uphold the fiction that the latter is Ernest.

Once alone, Jack furiously informs Algernon he will have to leave immediately. Algernon ignores these instructions and proceeds to court Cecily, declaring himself in love with her and asking her to marry him. Cecily surprises him with the news that they are already engaged. She has imagined all the details of their relationship and recorded them in her diary. Cecily is particularly delighted that her fiancé is named Ernest, a revelation that prompts Algernon to also seek re-christening. While he is arranging this business, Gwendolen arrives. She is surprised to discover the existence of Cecily, who informs the visitor that Ernest has a brother named Jack who acts as her guardian. Gwendolen is further taken aback when Cecily announces that she is herself engaged to Ernest. Gwendolen promptly makes her own claim to Ernest's hand in marriage. When Jack and Algernon appear, the women discover they are not in fact engaged to the same man. Their relief quickly turns to horror as they learn neither man is named Ernest.

In Act Three, Jack and Algernon announce their plans to be re-christened and the two couples are reconciled. Their happiness is short-lived as Lady Bracknell, having discovered Gwendolen's whereabouts, arrives. She disallows Jack's engagement to Gwendolen and questions him as to Cecily's identity. Upon her discovery of the girl's fortune Lady Bracknell warmly approves her engagement to Algernon. Jack, however, refuses to give his consent unless Lady Bracknell allows his own marriage to Gwendolen. Lady Bracknell will not agree to this and, as Cecily remains under Jack's guardianship until the age of thirty-five, the couples are at an impasse. Upon Dr Chasuble's arrival and mention of Miss Prism, Lady Bracknell demands to see the governess. She interrogates Miss Prism as to the whereabouts of a baby left in her charge twenty-eight years earlier. Miss Prism is unable to tell her, admitting she left the baby in a handbag at Victoria Station. Jack departs the room and returns with the handbag in question. He mistakenly assumes Miss Prism is his mother until Lady Bracknell informs him he is the son of her own sister and thus Algernon's elder brother. Lady Bracknell cannot remember his name beyond the fact that he was named after his father, the General. Jack consults the Army Lists, which show that the General's name was Ernest. The play closes with Jack and Gwendolen, and Algernon and Cecily, officially united and Miss Prism and Dr Chasuble confessing their love for one another.

Character summaries

John Worthing, J.P. (Jack, Ernest)

John Worthing, referred to as 'Jack', is the squire of the Manor House, an estate in the English county of Hertfordshire. He is a Justice of the Peace, which means he acts as a local magistrate in his home county. When in London, Jack poses as his younger brother 'Ernest', a name Lane, Algernon, Lady Bracknell and Gwendolen all know him by.

Algernon Moncrieff

Algernon Moncrieff is a young bachelor who lives in London. He is a friend of Jack's, and the nephew of Lady Bracknell and cousin of Gwendolen; at the end of the play we discover that he is Jack's brother. Algernon claims to have an invalid friend, 'Bunbury', who often needs his care.

Rev. Canon Frederick Chasuble, D.D.

Dr Chasuble is canon of the parish within which Jack's country estate is located. He is a Doctor of Divinity (D.D.) and thus has undertaken advanced study in theology.

Merriman

Merriman is employed as the butler at the Manor House.

Lane

Lane is Algernon's manservant, based at the latter's flat in Half-Moon Street.

Lady Bracknell

Lady Bracknell is wife of the unseen Lord Bracknell, mother of Gwendolen and aunt of Algernon. She is a formidable Society matron, based in London.

Hon. Gwendolen Fairfax

Gwendolen is the daughter of Lady Bracknell and potential fiancée of Jack. The term 'Hon.' (short for 'Honourable') indicates that she is a member of the aristocracy.

Cecily Cardew

Eighteen-year-old Cecily lives at the Manor House under Jack's guardianship. She was entrusted to his care by her late grandfather, Mr Thomas Cardew.

Miss Laetitia Prism

Miss Prism lives at the Manor House, where she is employed as Cecily's governess. She was previously in service to the Moncrieff family in London.

BACKGROUND & CONTEXT

Class and 'Society'

Individuals in nineteenth-century England were organised into social classes. Class was defined by occupation, family connections and access to wealth. Individuals generally remained within the class they were born into. At the top of the scale were the upper class, consisting of the aristocracy, the landed gentry and a select number of wealthy professionals and manufacturers. At the pinnacle of the upper class were the members of 'Society', a social enclave (district) centred around the royal court. The middle class was represented by professionals (including doctors, lawyers and bankers), manufacturers, artists and retailers. The working classes consisted of domestic servants, tradespeople, retail workers and labourers. The poor and destitute existed outside this framework but remained visible and a significant source of anxiety.

Several classes are represented in *The Importance of Being Earnest*. Lane, Merriman and the footman who appears briefly in Scene 10 belong to the working class; Miss Prism and Dr Chasuble are part of the genteel middle class; and Jack, Algernon, Gwendolen, Lady Bracknell and Cecily are members of the upper class. (Note: Wilde's text is not divided into scenes; Scene 10 here refers to the scene divisions used in this guide. See the Scene-by-scene analysis for the outlines of these scenes.)

Wilde's play can be read as a satire of the class system, particularly of the upper-class elite who formed 'Society'. Society was structured around social rituals, and governed by the strict rules of etiquette. The most significant rituals were those surrounding birth, coming-of-age, marriage and death: all of which are depicted or mentioned in the play.

Although the upper classes still retained immense power and privilege in the late nineteenth century, the distribution of wealth had changed in the wake of the Industrial Revolution. The development and expansion of new industries such as mining and manufacturing brought wealth to people outside the upper classes, and increasing numbers of people were moving up the social scale. The aristocracy responded with some anxiety to this development and used the rules of etiquette as a means of policing entry to Society.

The growing numbers of people in the middle classes also meant the values and preoccupations of this class became more prominent, spreading throughout society and influencing all spheres of life. These values included respectability, earnestness, thrift, duty, self-improvement and piety. Miss Prism is an obvious representative of such values.

Significantly, *The Importance of Being Earnest* was first presented at the St James's Theatre in London, perhaps the most fashionable theatre of its time. The St James's attracted the most glittering and aristocratic members of Society, as well as many leading intellectuals and artists. It was also attended by lower-middle and working-class patrons; however, they were relegated to the back of the theatre. The focus in the auditorium was on Society. The upper-class theatregoers saw their world reflected back at them onstage at the St James's. This was especially the case with Wilde's play, to the extent that one reviewer suggested middle- and working-class patrons experienced it as a sightseeing trip into the world of Society: 'The people in the humbler parts of the house evidently keenly enjoyed the graphic glimpses which the dramatist gave them of the inner life of those "higher ranks"' (Donohue and Berggren 1995, p.281).

The *fin de siècle*

The period in which *The Importance of Being Earnest* appeared, the late nineteenth century, is sometimes referred to as the *fin de siècle*: a French term that literally means 'end of the century'. The *fin de siècle* was characterised by a loss of confidence and a sense of impending doom, prompted by factors such as threats to British imperialism, economic competition from abroad, political turmoil at home and social upheaval as conventions of class and gender were challenged. We can see these preoccupations reflected in *The Importance of Being Earnest*. In the 'tea scene' in Act Two, Cecily taunts Gwendolen with the spectre of 'agricultural depression', noting: 'I believe the aristocracy are suffering very much from it just at present' (p.337). When Gwendolen learns of Jack and Algernon's plans to be re-christened she praises their bravery by exclaiming, 'How absurd to talk of the equality of the sexes! Where questions of self-sacrifice are concerned, men are infinitely beyond us' (p.346). Her attitude to gender relations mocks the language and attitudes of nineteenth-century feminists. This example highlights the way the characters in the play repeatedly trivialise serious issues. The target of the satire is not so much the serious issue – in this case gender equality – as it is Gwendolen's attitude, which suggests the isolation and self-absorption of many upper-class individuals.

Aestheticism and Decadence

Oscar Wilde was associated with two artistic movements that achieved prominence in the 1880s and 1890s – Aestheticism and Decadence. Aestheticism is the commitment to beauty, the celebration of beauty as its own reward. Supporters of this movement held that art did not need to have a purpose, offer social commentary or provide instruction it could and should be judged on its own terms. The Aesthetic movement was inspired by the work of critic Walter Pater, who wrote in 1873 of 'the desire for beauty, the love of art for its own sake' (Abrams 1993, p.1534). This notion of 'art for art's sake' became the catchcry of the Aesthetic movement.

The preface to Wilde's novel, *The Picture of Dorian Gray*, was read as the manifesto of the Aesthetic movement. In it, Wilde made pronouncements such as:

- 'There is no such thing as a moral or an immoral book. Books are well written, or badly written. That is all.' (Abrams 1993, p.1628)
- 'We can forgive a man for making a useful thing as long as he does not admire it. The only excuse for making a useless thing is that one admires it intensely.' (Abrams 1993, p.1628)

Taking the Aesthetic philosophy to its extreme demanded that one treat life itself as art. We see this attitude reflected throughout *The Importance of Being Earnest*. For example, Cecily and Gwendolen's diaries frame the details of their lives like works of fiction (Cecily's diary is 'meant for publication', p.329; Gwendolen claims the content of her diary is 'sensational', p.336). Similarly, Algernon criticises 'people who are not serious about meals' (p.303). In Algernon's opinion, eating should be afforded the kind of sustained consideration an art critic might give to a painting.

The Decadent movement was closely related to Aestheticism but took some of its ideas further. It was a darker and, for many observers, a more sinister and troubling philosophy. While mainstream Victorians valued vigour, drive, morality and charity, the Decadents championed languor (lack of energy), boredom, perversity and hedonism (the pursuit of pleasure). They delighted in art and artifice and rejected anything 'natural'. They experimented with masks, cosmetics and costumes as a means of manipulating nature, and revelled in performance and posing. They challenged gender roles and celebrated androgyny and sexual ambiguity. The Decadents were also interested in the grotesque, a form that brings together opposites such as 'natural' and 'artificial', or 'male' and 'female', to unsettle the spectator.

Wilde's own commitment to style and artifice was symbolised in his wearing a green carnation in the buttonhole of his suit – green carnations do not grow naturally. The green carnation became a symbol of Decadence, of art attempting to 'outdo' nature.

Q How are the philosophies of Aestheticism and Decadence reflected in the play?

Production of the text

For a play about multiple identities, it is appropriate that there is actually more than one version of *The Importance of Being Earnest*. Its first incarnation surfaced in mid 1894, when Wilde wrote to George Alexander, actor-manager of the St James's Theatre, about a new three-act play he was writing. The scenario was essentially the same as that of the version we have today, although nearly all the characters had different names – Ernest was George – and there was no handbag. In October 1894, Wilde sent Alexander the manuscript of this play, which he had titled *Lady Lancing*. Wilde had extended the play to four acts but Alexander urged him to condense it back into three. Under the title *The Importance of Being Earnest,* Wilde's play opened at the St James's Theatre on 14 February 1895. The four-act version, which includes two extra characters (a solicitor and a gardener), still exists as a kind of phantom alternative *Earnest*. The deleted scene in which the solicitor, Gribsby, arrives at Jack's country house to arrest Ernest for unpaid bills is included as an appendix to the Penguin Classics edition (pp.359–63).

The first edition of *The Importance of Being Earnest* was published in 1899, after Wilde had been released from prison. The playwright himself supervised the publication and made slight changes to the manuscript, some of these based on developments that occurred in the original production.

GENRE, STRUCTURE & LANGUAGE

The Importance of Being Earnest borrows from a number of theatrical forms, including the comedy of manners, farce, melodrama and the problem play.

Satire

Satire is the use of comic techniques to ridicule a folly or vice. Although the Victorian age is generally thought of as one of high seriousness, it produced a wealth of satirical writings exposing the hypocrisy and pomposity of the period as well as ridiculing the latest fads and fashions. In the late nineteenth century such works included the operas of WS Gilbert, the comic magazine *Punch* and the verse of Edward Lear and Lewis Carroll.

The Importance of Being Earnest satirises a range of Victorian subjects, including:

- the emphasis on appearances
- Victorian attitudes to morality
- the importance of 'name' and parentage
- British prejudices and assumptions about other nations and their culture, in particular France and Germany.

As well as satirising Victorian values and prejudices, *The Importance of Being Earnest* also parodies dramatic forms such as melodrama and the problem play (see below).

Q What other targets of satire can you identify in the text?

Comedy of manners

The comedy of manners is a dramatic form that gained prominence in the eighteenth century. In this form the comedy derives from the manners and mores (customs and conventions) of a particular social group, most often the ruling elite. These plays are commonly set in the homes of the well-to-do and depict their social rituals, such as visiting calls and courtship. In doing so, the comedy of manners exposes their prejudices and assumptions for ridicule. We can see this technique in Wilde's depiction of the pretensions of Lady Bracknell, such as her assessment of Cecily's facial profile in Scene 13. Lady Bracknell advises her: 'The chin a little higher, dear. Style largely depends on the way the chin is worn. They are worn very high, just at present' (p.349). Such comments exaggerate Society's focus on appearances to the point of nonsense, making Lady Bracknell's values and strictures – and those of the social group she represents – look absurd.

Farce

Farce was popular throughout the nineteenth century and continues to influence entertainment forms today. Victorian farces employed visual gags and slapstick humour, and featured fast-paced comic narratives of mistaken identity, misunderstandings and coincidences. *The Importance of Being Earnest* is farcical in its use of confusion and misunderstandings as the basis of much of its humour; however, it departs from farce in the style of performance it requires. In a farce, actors are suspended between the world of the play and the world of the audience: they signal to the audience that they are aware of the innuendo in their dialogue and the absurdity of their characters and situations. In comparison, *The Importance of Being Earnest* should be played with absolute seriousness. The actors must completely inhabit the world of the play. This approach goes against the instinct of most actors when appearing in comedy. Even the actor Sir John Gielgud, recognised as a master of Wildean comedy, 'realized only toward the end of his career that the muffin-eating sequence should be played slowly, "with real solemnity"' (Raby 1988, p.123).

Melodrama

Melodrama is the form most often associated with the Victorian theatre. These plays featured formulaic plots of good versus evil; a cast of stock characters (the hero, the villain, the damsel); and a happy ending. Resolutions would often be effected through the discovery of a character's mistaken identity. For example, it would be revealed that the noble peasant was actually the squire's son and stands to inherit the property from which he is being evicted.

Victorian melodrama was intensely sentimental. In its depiction of untimely deaths and mother-and-child reunions, it worked to provoke an emotional response in the audience. Such events occur in *The Importance of Being Earnest* (for example, Jack's announcement of Ernest's death from a 'severe chill', p.323; Jack's reunion with Miss Prism, p.355), but they are framed comically. In melodrama, love is always constant and true love always triumphs. Such constancy is subverted in Wilde's play: Cecily and Gwendolen promise to love truly, madly, deeply, forever – but only if your name is Ernest.

A key feature of melodrama is the use of names to indicate character traits. In *The Importance of Being Earnest*, this technique is particularly apparent in the characters of Miss Prism, Dr Chasuble and Jack Worthing. 'Miss Prism' sounds like a synthesis of 'prissy' and 'prim', words that could be used to describe this character. 'Miss Prism' also suggests the word 'misprision', meaning a mistake or wrongful act or, in legal terms, an act of negligence. Taken in this sense her name recalls her actions relating to the loss of baby Jack at the train station. A 'chasuble' is a priestly vestment worn by some Anglican clergymen in the nineteenth century. The word also sounds similar to chastity. 'Worthing' is not just a reference to a seaside resort; it also signals Jack's character – he is serious, grave, 'worthy' (or, at least, maintains the appearance of such attributes), as befitting a Justice of the Peace.

The problem play

In the early part of the nineteenth century, theatres were large, noisy venues patronised by a predominantly working-class audience. Later in the century more intimate, decorous spaces were built as part of an effort to encourage middle- and upper-class patrons into the theatre. Playwrights developed new dramatic forms reflecting the interests and preoccupations of the middle and upper classes. One such form was the 'Society Drama', with characters drawn from the aristocracy. As society was changing rapidly in the 1890s, playwrights increasingly explored moral issues or problems through drama; such works became known as 'problem plays'. The problem play presented more complex, psychologically motivated characters than those that appeared in melodrama. Wilde's plays *Lady Windermere's Fan*, *A Woman of No Importance* and *An Ideal Husband* are versions of the society drama and problem play. *The Importance of Being Earnest* can be read as a parody of these forms.

Structure

The play is divided into three acts. Act One is set in London; Acts Two and Three are set a day or two later and move the action to the country. The logical place for an interval is after Act One, to indicate the passage of time and change of location. For ease of discussion, I have divided the action into fourteen scenes (see the Scene-by-scene analysis for more detail).

There is structural symmetry to the play. The characters form pairs or 'doubles': Jack and Algernon; Gwendolen and Cecily; Miss Prism and Dr Chasuble; Lane and Merriman. Only Lady Bracknell stands alone, thereby enhancing her impact and her individuality. There are also symmetries within the plot: both bachelors have imaginary friends that help them lead double lives; both men kill off their imaginary friends in the course of the play; both men propose; both of the women they propose to favour the name 'Ernest'. This mirroring structure heightens the sense of artificiality. As Richard Allen Cave notes in his Introduction to the Penguin Classics edition, the use of mirroring advances to the extent that, in Scene 12, 'the dialogue for each couple exactly mirrors the responses of the other pair to the point where both men and the women begin speaking together in unison' (p.xviii).

Language

The Importance of Being Earnest is distinguished by its use of language. The poet WH Auden described the play as 'the only pure verbal opera in English' (Raby 1988, p.120). This is a text that should be spoken aloud to feel the rhythm of the sentences. Wilde uses phrasing to create rhythm. Note how the inclusion of a single word ('just') in a sentence such as 'I believe the aristocracy are suffering very much from it just at present' (Cecily, p.337) changes the tempo of the line.

The play uses a number of specific literary techniques to build comedy, including the following devices.

Epigram

This is a short, sharp, witty phrase. Wilde was a master of the epigram in both life and literature. He often recycled epigrams in several works. For example, Gwendolen's comments in Scene 12, 'In matters of grave importance, style, not sincerity, is the vital thing' (p.345), appeared in Wilde's earlier essay 'Phrases and Philosophies for the Use of the Young' (1894).

Algernon frequently uses epigrams. Some examples include:

- 'All women become like their mothers. That is their tragedy. No man does. That's his.' (p.312)
- 'The only way to behave to a woman is to make love to her, if she is pretty, and to someone else if she is plain.' (p.313)

Q How does Wilde use epigrams to convey a sense of Algernon's character? Note also when and with whom Algernon uses epigrams and how his language changes with Lady Bracknell and, in particular, Cecily.

Paradox

Paradox is the technique of combining apparently contradictory terms, characteristics or values. Gwendolen, in particular, uses paradox in her dialogue. Some examples include:

- 'The simplicity of your character makes you exquisitely incomprehensible to me.' (p.315)
- 'And certainly once a man begins to neglect his domestic duties he becomes painfully effeminate, does he not?' (p.334)
- 'If you are not too long, I will wait here for you all my life.' (p.354)

Q Why might the technique of paradox be particularly appropriate for Gwendolen?

Puns

A pun is the use of language to make a play on words. It exploits the sound or meaning of a word for comic effect. A classic example of punning occurs in Scene 2:

> Jack: My dear Algy, you talk exactly as if you were a dentist. It is very vulgar to talk like a dentist when one isn't a dentist. It produces a false impression.
>
> Algernon: Well, that is exactly what dentists always do. (p.300)

The pun here plays on the double meaning of the word 'impression' as both 'to produce an effect upon' and a dentist's mould of the teeth.

The title of the play is also a pun. Jack repeats the title in the play's final line: 'I've now realized for the first time in my life the vital Importance of Being Earnest' (p.358). The pun exploits the fact that the name 'Ernest' is a homophone (a word with the same sound but different meaning) of the word 'earnest'.

Q An audience hearing this line would not know whether Jack was referring to the name or the quality. How do you think they would interpret it? What do you think Wilde is exposing through this pun?

SCENE-BY-SCENE ANALYSIS

Note: in the ***Key vocabulary*** sections I have only provided definitions for words and phrases not included in Richard Allen Cave's notes to the Penguin Classics edition.

Each act is divided into scenes for ease of discussion; these scenes begin and end at the page numbers given, with the exit or entrance of a character. Page references are for the Penguin Classics edition of the play.

Act One, Scene 1 (pp.295–6)

Summary: *Algernon and his manservant Lane discuss preparations for the arrival of Lady Bracknell.*

The opening scene ushers us into a world of class privilege. The first action in the play shows the servant Lane tending his master's flat in the fashionable London district of Mayfair. Algernon himself is established as an idle bachelor whose chief preoccupations in life are eating and pleasure-seeking.

The topsy-turvy philosophical perspective of the play is revealed in the interaction between these two characters, as seemingly trivial concerns – such as cucumber sandwiches – are treated with greater seriousness than issues and institutions – such as marriage – which conventionally hold more importance.

The scene closes with an example of Wilde's use of inversion as Algernon comments, 'Really, if the lower orders don't set us a good example, what on earth is the use of them?' (p.296). The expected term in such a phrase would be *upper* orders, drawing on the notion that the privileged members of society have a duty to act responsibly and set a good example. The substitution of 'lower' for 'upper' makes us laugh but also invites us to question the validity of the original proposition, to ask *why* the upper orders should be held as a good example for the less privileged.

Key point

The opening scene uses language and visual signs to establish the setting of the play: the upper-class society of late-Victorian England. Note, for example, the description of the flat; Lane's position in the household; and the references to luxuries such as expensive champagne.

Q How would you describe Algernon's and Lane's attitudes to each other? What do these attitudes suggest about class relations?

Scene 2 (pp.296–303)

Summary: *Jack arrives at Algernon's flat; Algernon presents the cigarette case; Jack's double identity is revealed.*

Upon his arrival at Algernon's flat, Jack is introduced as 'Mr Ernest Worthing' (p.296). When Jack reveals his plans to propose to Algernon's cousin Gwendolen, Algernon is prompted to produce Ernest's cigarette case, which was left at his house.

Key point

The appearance of the cigarette case is facilitated by Lane, as is the announcement of 'Ernest' and the later arrival of Lady Bracknell and Gwendolen. This establishes a pattern that continues throughout the play, whereby the actions of the principal characters are 'stage-managed' by their servants.

Algernon's presentation of the cigarette case reveals that 'Ernest' is in fact 'Jack', a double identity that Algernon equates with his own creation of the invalid friend, Bunbury: 'I may mention that I have always suspected you of being a confirmed and secret Bunburyist; and I am quite sure of it now' (p.300). Through these imaginary entities the men are able to evade responsibility. Algernon is relieved of attendance at social events by the need to minister to the ailing Bunbury; Jack escapes the restrictions of his country estate, including guardianship of his ward Cecily, and pursues a life of pleasure-seeking in London by posing as his fictitious brother

Ernest. Much of the chaos – and humour – of the play will stem from Jack and Algernon's dependence on these fictive 'doubles'.

Key point

The play invites questions about the nature and value of truth and honesty. Neither Jack nor Algernon can maintain his current lifestyle without resorting to deception; each man can only be 'true' to himself and his desires through a complex series of lies.

Q What are the differences between Jack and Algernon? What do they have in common? Why are they friends?

Scene 3 (pp.303–7)

Summary: *Lady Bracknell and Gwendolen arrive at Algernon's flat; Jack proposes to Gwendolen.*

This scene introduces us to the formidable Lady Bracknell and her fashionable daughter, Gwendolen. Lady Bracknell's conversation reveals the pastimes and preoccupations of the Society matron: her life is a round of receptions, dinner parties, visiting calls – and gossip. The obligations of a bachelor nephew, such as Algernon, within this world are also outlined and the benefits of having a 'Bunbury' become more evident. Algernon cannot escape all responsibility, however; to maintain favour he must fulfil some duties, such as arranging the music at his aunt's forthcoming reception. Lady Bracknell exerts her influence even here, stressing the propriety of German music over French: 'French songs I cannot possibly allow ... But German sounds a thoroughly respectable language' (p.305). Her comments satirise English prejudices, whereby French culture was associated with decadence and immorality and German with earnestness and intellectualism. Lady Bracknell's attitude demonstrates the importance of surface in this world. She doesn't really care what the music is about, so long as it *sounds* respectable.

Algernon works within the bounds of etiquette and convention to achieve his desires. Gwendolen also manipulates convention for her own ends. She takes the dominant role in Jack's attempt to propose to her, manoeuvring the conversation in the direction of her choice. Having advised him to propose before her mother returns she adds, 'I think it only fair to tell you quite frankly beforehand that I am fully determined to accept you' (p.307). Gwendolen is a striking contrast to the conventional Victorian girl, who was typically depicted as naive, unassuming and passive. Gwendolen is knowing, forthright and determined. Even so, she remains a servant of convention, guiding Jack in the proper form of a proposal even as she reveals the entire incident to be a highly choreographed performance.

The importance of form over feeling is further demonstrated by Gwendolen's reaction to Jack's given name which she believes is Ernest: 'my ideal has always been to love someone of the name of Ernest. There is something in that name that inspires absolute confidence' (p.306). Her determination to marry an 'Ernest' is so absolute and unwavering that Jack resolves to have himself re-christened rather than reveal the truth of his identity. His reaction is comical; however, it also suggests the importance of 'name' in Victorian society, an issue that comes to the fore in the next scene when Lady Bracknell discovers that Jack does not actually know his birth name.

Q What attracts Jack and Gwendolen to each other?

Key vocabulary

Ready money: cash.

The season: the time of year when Society held its most important social engagements, including the presentation of debutantes (girls aged eighteen) to the reigning monarch at court. The season extended from February to August but was at its height between May and June.

Scene 4 (pp.308–11)

Summary: *Lady Bracknell discovers Jack's uncertain origins and forbids his marriage to her daughter.*

When Lady Bracknell returns to the room, Gwendolen informs her that she and Jack are engaged. Lady Bracknell refutes this notion and orders Gwendolen to the carriage.

The centrepiece of this act, and one of the key scenes of the play, is Lady Bracknell's interview with Jack, in which she assesses his suitability as a husband for Gwendolen. Lady Bracknell's catalogue of questions covers the areas of importance in a prospective marriage suit: education, pursuits and finances. Her responses to his answers, however, satirise Victorian mores. When Jack admits he smokes, she remarks, 'I am glad to hear it. A man should always have an occupation of some kind. There are far too many idle men in London as it is' (p.308). Lady Bracknell's response makes fun of the Victorian imperative to be busy and useful.

The interchange reaches the heights of absurdity in Jack's revelation of his beginnings in a handbag in a cloakroom at Victoria Station: 'I don't actually know who I am by birth. I was ... well, I was found' and 'I was in a hand-bag – a somewhat large, black leather hand-bag, with handles to it' (p.310). He tries to bolster his case by adding details, noting that he was found in a station on the Brighton line. Lady Bracknell is unimpressed: the 'line is immaterial' she replies (p.311), a response that puns on the double meaning of the word as both a train route and a family tree. It is not so much the particulars of his origins as his inability to 'prove his name' – to provide evidence of his family lineage – that causes Lady Bracknell to terminate the interview and disallow the engagement.

Q What rules and preoccupations of Society are revealed in this scene?

Key vocabulary

Duties exacted from one after one's death: 'death duties' was the colloquial term for taxes applied to deceased estates.

Tories: supporters of conservative politics.

Scene 5 (pp.311–16)

Summary: *Jack plots to kill Ernest; Gwendolen reiterates her devotion to Jack; Algernon plans a spot of Bunburying.*

The final scene of Act One prepares the audience for the plot developments of Act Two. In an attempt to simplify his life, Jack proposes to kill Ernest, being careful to choose a method of death – 'a severe chill' (p.313) – that will not reflect negatively on his own constitution. Much of the scene is made up of banter between Jack and Algernon, for example:

> Algernon: What shall we do after dinner? Go to a theatre?
> Jack: Oh, no! I loathe listening.
> Algernon: Well, let us go to the Club?
> Jack: Oh, no! I hate talking.
> Algernon: Well, we might trot round to the Empire at ten?
> Jack: Oh, no! I can't bear looking at things. It is so silly. (p.314)

This exchange offers a further example of the men's style of communication and suggests their characters and concerns. Does it also perhaps invite criticism of the aimlessness of their existence?

Gwendolen makes a sudden return to assure Jack that her feelings for him have not been lessened by his unfortunate interview with her mother. Her return allows Jack to give her his country address, a conversation that is overhead by Algernon. The stage direction tells us Algernon '*smiles to himself, and writes the address on his shirt-cuff. Then picks up the Railway Guide*' (p.315). This moment demonstrates the importance of non-verbal communication in the play. The stage direction clearly indicates Algernon's plans to complicate matters by descending on the country estate and introducing himself to Cecily, whom he has already expressed a desire to meet ('I would rather like to see Cecily', p.313), without his having to say a word.

Q Why does Jack not want Algernon to meet Cecily?

Q Note Jack's repeated use of the word 'nonsense' in this scene. What is his attitude to 'nonsense'? How does this compare to Algernon's attitude?

Key vocabulary

Apoplexy: a sudden fit brought on by a stroke.

Ward: a child or adolescent who has been entrusted to an adult guardian's care following the death or incapacity of their parents.

Act Two, Scene 6 (pp.317–22)

Summary: *Introduction of Cecily and Miss Prism; Dr Chasuble rescues Cecily from her lesson; Algernon appears as 'Mr Ernest Worthing'.*

Act Two transplants the action of the play to Jack's country estate. The act opens on an idyllic summer scene, with Jack's ward, Cecily, and her governess, Miss Prism, in the garden. Miss Prism calls Cecily away from watering the flowers: 'Cecily, Cecily! Surely such a utilitarian occupation as the watering of flowers is rather Moulton's duty than yours?' (p.317). This comment gives us an insight into the activities considered appropriate for a Victorian girl. She was expected to be busy and useful but not to undertake duties considered below her station, such as housework or gardening. Rather, she should devote herself to charitable works and self-improvement.

Cecily and Miss Prism's firm belief in Jack's moral authority is also underscored in this scene. Miss Prism knows of 'no one who has a higher sense of duty and responsibility' (p.317). Such comments are ironic as the audience is already aware of Jack's double identity.

As we have been expecting since witnessing him copy the address of Jack's country estate, Algernon arrives to visit Cecily. Less expected is his choice to pose as the fictional Ernest. The ensuing dialogue shows Cecily's well-formulated idea of Ernest's character: 'You, I see from your card, are Uncle Jack's brother, my cousin Ernest, my wicked cousin Ernest' (p.320). Cecily delights in the notion of Ernest's wickedness. In common with Gwendolen's display of knowingness and determination in Act One, Cecily's characterisation resists Victorian stereotypes of girls as retiring and passive. The use of inversion in her dialogue produces effective comedy: 'I hope you have not been leading a double life, pretending to be wicked and being really good all the time. That would be hypocrisy' (p.320). Cecily's line also satirises the Victorian emphasis on surface: the idea that the *appearance* of morality is more important than true goodness.

This scene reveals that Jack had been thinking of ridding himself of Ernest prior to proposing to Gwendolen. Cecily tells Algernon of Jack's plans for him: 'Well, he said at dinner on Wednesday night, that you would have to choose between this world, the next world and Australia' (p.321). Emigration to Britain's colonies was considered a suitable way of dealing with errant individuals, particularly aimless younger brothers.

Q Compare the activities, values and language of the country characters with those of the city characters.

Key vocabulary

Three-volume novel: in the early nineteenth century, novels were published in three volumes. As books were expensive, many readers relied on circulating libraries (such as the Mudie library referred to here); publishing a novel in three volumes meant more copies could be lent to readers. As printing processes became less expensive this practice decreased and the 'three-volume novel' became associated with an outmoded style of fiction.

Scene 7 (pp.322–5)

Summary: *Jack announces Ernest's death; Dr Chasuble agrees to christen Jack.*

Wilde's ability to build visual humour emerges again in this act, as Jack appears in mourning dress. Victorian custom demanded bereaved relatives observe a period of mourning following a death in the family. This involved wearing simple, unadorned black clothing and avoiding social events. Jack's appearance in mourning demonstrates the extent of his fiction and its effects on those around him.

Humour arises in the audience's knowledge that Jack is observing mourning for the very individual Cecily has just greeted and invited into the house ('Ernest'). Jack's entrance produced a terrific sensation on the opening night of the first production. Critic William Archer noted, 'as [Jack] marches solemnly down the stage, and before a word is spoken, you can feel the idea kindling from row to row, until a sudden glory of laughter fills the theatre' (Donohue and Berggren 1995, p.225). George Alexander, the actor playing Jack, emphasised the joke by taking out 'a large black-bordered handkerchief' (Jackson 1980, p.51) and dabbing his eyes on the line 'Poor Ernest! He had many faults, but it is a sad, sad blow' (p.323).

Q How would the absence of these kinds of mourning rituals in today's society influence an audience's appreciation of this scene?

Key vocabulary

Misanthrope and womanthrope: a misanthrope is an individual who hates humankind or, as it would have been referred to in the Victorian era, mankind. Miss Prism makes a play on this meaning, suggesting that rather than hating *man*kind, Dr Chasuble hates *woman*kind. The correct word for such a person is *misogynist*.

Neologistic: a neologism is a word or phrase that has only recently been invented; Dr Chasuble uses the word with reference to Miss Prism's creation of the term 'womanthrope', a playful use of language to which he reacts '*with a scholar's shudder*' (p.322).

Scene 8 (pp.325–8)

Summary: *Jack and Ernest are reconciled; Jack calls the dog-cart to take Algernon to the station.*

Jack has quite a self-satisfied air at the beginning of this scene, having, as he believes, neatly freed himself from his brother and made arrangements for his own re-christening. He is soon deflated, however, by the sudden reappearance of Ernest in the person of Algernon. This scene cleverly balances the characters' conflicting perspectives for comic effect: setting Jack's anger and discomfort against Cecily's happiness, Miss Prism and Dr Chasuble's confusion and Algernon's glee.

The remainder of the scene offers further examples of Algernon's ability to manipulate a situation to his personal advantage and thwart Jack's desires. The pattern of the dialogue demonstrates Algernon's control and Jack's frustration. Jack's petty, biting comments have no effect; Algernon effortlessly returns Jack's barbs or transforms them into compliments. Jack uses every weapon at his disposal. He tells Algernon, 'Your duty as a gentleman calls you back' (p.327), thus striking at the heart of Victorian masculinity. The 'gentleman' was a complex label but one that every right-thinking Victorian man aspired to hold. The gentleman was independently wealthy, of good family, noble character and refined manners. Algernon is untroubled by Jack's attack on his character: 'My duty as a gentleman has never interfered with my pleasures in the smallest degree' (p.327). The dialogue shows the two men as doubles, cancelling out the actions of each other; as one man's desire is thwarted, the other's is realised.

Key vocabulary

Portmanteau: suitcase.

Scene 9 (pp.328–32)

Summary: *Algernon cancels the dog-cart; Algernon discovers his engagement to Cecily.*

In this scene Algernon, posing as Ernest, attempts to sweet-talk Cecily, only to discover she and Ernest have already established a relationship. Cecily has created an imaginary courtship with Ernest and recorded the details in her diary. This scene mirrors the earlier one between Jack and Gwendolen, with the female partner taking the dominant role in the relationship.

Cecily has constructed her imaginary partnership with Ernest around conventional romantic emblems: they were engaged on St Valentine's

Day; she keeps his letters tied with a blue ribbon; she wears a 'little bangle with the true lover's knot' (p.330). Yet our sense of her as a conventional romantic heroine is complicated by her obvious power – she has brought the relationship into existence and directs its course. She is also far from self-effacing or retiring: she takes delight in 'being looked at' (p.334) and her diary is 'meant for publication' (p.329).

These characters are brought to action, and find meaning, less through the material demands of the real world than through the elaborate fictions they create. Cecily is bored by her lessons, but animated by her fantasy life. Algernon (himself an embellisher of real life) falls for the power of her imagination.

In a further mirroring of the interaction between Jack and Gwendolen, Cecily expresses her delight in the prospect of marrying a man named, as she believes, Ernest. The two women use almost identical words to make this point: Gwendolen says that 'there is something in that name that inspires absolute confidence' (p.306), and Cecily observes, 'there is something in that name that seems to inspire absolute confidence' (p.332). This is the first moment in the play where we see Algernon genuinely disconcerted. As befits their status as 'doubles', his response to the problem is identical to Jack's: he must be re-christened.

Q Is Algernon reformed by Cecily? How do you account for his sudden change of attitude to marriage?

Q What similarities and differences can you identify between Cecily and Gwendolen? Compare, for example, their attitudes to romance and marriage.

Scene 10 (pp.333–40)

Summary: *Gwendolen and Cecily discover they are both engaged to Ernest; Jack and Algernon's deception is revealed.*

Further complicating matters, Gwendolen arrives at Jack's country house. The sudden appearance of a character believed to be safely located elsewhere enhances the farcical tone of Act Two.

Gwendolen and Cecily quickly fulfil Jack's prediction by calling each other 'sister' (p.339); however, this only happens, as Algernon foresaw, after 'they have called each other a lot of other things first' (p.314). Although they begin by observing standard social niceties, the two women soon exchange more serious information. There are the revelations of Cecily's identity as Mr Worthing's ward; of the existence of Ernest Worthing's brother; and of the fact both women are engaged to Ernest. Cecily and Gwendolen mirror each other in their responses to the final disclosure – attempting to subtly undercut the other before resorting to outright attack. Gwendolen asks, 'do you allude to me, Miss Cardew, as an entanglement? You are presumptuous', and Cecily asks in response, 'do you suggest, Miss Fairfax, that I entrapped Ernest into an engagement? How dare you?' (p.336).

This entire pattern of civility escalating into accusation is repeated when Merriman serves tea and they are forced back behind a facade of politeness. The tea scene exploits visual humour as Cecily serves Gwendolen cake and adds sugar to her tea, in express contradiction of the guest's requests (p.337). This moment of pantomime gives Cecily the upper hand and fuels the bitter attack that follows.

The animosity between the two women is dissolved as Jack and Algernon arrive and their true identities are revealed. Cecily and Gwendolen are subsequently united in their shared status as 'wronged woman': a recognised figure in Victorian literature. It is at this point that Jack's prediction is realised and Gwendolen asks Cecily, 'You will call me sister, will you not?' (p.339).

Q How are manners used as weapons in this scene?

Q Why has Wilde included the character of the footman in this scene? What does his presence contribute that the figure of Merriman alone would not? How might the two women modify their behaviour in the face of his presence?

Scene 11 (pp.340–3)

Summary: *Jack and Algernon argue over the muffins.*

The final scene of Act Two mirrors that of Act One, with Jack and Algernon reflecting on immediate developments and engaging in their usual banter. Algernon is amused at the turn of events: it is 'the most wonderful Bunbury I have ever had in my life' (p.340). Jack, however, is in a state of increasing irritation. He has only one effective means of provoking Algernon – withholding food from him – which prompts their spat over the muffins (note that these are English toasting muffins rather than the American cake-like muffins). The childish wrangling over the muffins resembles two brothers fighting over a toy, suggesting the true nature of Jack and Algernon's relationship, which is finally revealed in Act Three.

Q Why do the men move between calling their fiancées by their first names and full names in this scene?

Act Three, Scene 12 (pp.344–6)

Summary: *Jack and Algernon join Gwendolen and Cecily in the morning-room; the couples are reconciled.*

The action of Act Three takes place in a living room in Jack's country house. When Jack and Algernon join Gwendolen and Cecily they flatter the two women and fulfil their romantic expectations, thus moving closer to reconciliation. The extent of the doubling in this scene is evidenced in the women's articulation of the final obstacle to their forgiveness, and the men's replies:

> Gwendolen and Cecily [*speaking together*]: Your Christian names are still an insuperable barrier. That is all!
>
> Jack and Algernon [*speaking together*]: Our Christian names! Is that all? But we are going to be christened this afternoon. (p.345)

As the scene closes, it mocks codes of romance by framing the men's willingness to be re-christened as the kind of heroic endeavour a man must undergo to win his damsel. The use of the language of heroic chivalry heightens the absurdity of the situation, for example when Gwendolen says, 'how absurd to talk of the equality of the sexes! Where questions of self-sacrifice are concerned, men are infinitely beyond us' (p.346).

Scene 13 (pp.346–52)

Summary: *Lady Bracknell arrives; Algernon announces his engagement to Cecily; Jack refuses to give his consent to Algernon and Cecily's marriage; Lady Bracknell and Gwendolen prepare to leave.*

Lady Bracknell's sudden arrival thwarts the resolution effected in the previous scene. She maintains a supercilious (patronising) attitude towards Cecily, using the latter's engagement to Algernon as an opportunity for further jibes at Jack's origins, until Jack reveals the fact of the girl's fortune. At this news, Lady Bracknell warms to Cecily and assesses her 'social possibilities' (p.349). Her attitude is indicative of her mercenary nature and that of Society in general: personal gain is always a priority.

Key point

In this scene, Lady Bracknell discloses an extremely telling piece of information: 'When I married Lord Bracknell I had no fortune of any kind. But I never dreamed for a moment of allowing that to stand in my way' (p.349). This suggests Lady Bracknell is a social climber and perhaps originally an outsider, as indicated by the fact that she is the only character without a double.

Just as Jack is only able to manipulate Algernon through access to food, so, too, he is only able to gain some power over Lady Bracknell through access to money. Jack refuses to give his consent for Cecily's marriage to Algernon unless Lady Bracknell will allow his own marriage to Gwendolen. This is significant as, in a beautifully ridiculous plot development, Jack reveals that Cecily will not 'come of age' and become legally responsible for her own decisions until she is thirty-five (the usual age was twenty-one). Jack's moment of power is short-lived, however, as Lady Bracknell refuses to trade Gwendolen's hand in marriage. The scene closes with Lady Bracknell again in the position of power and the couples at an impasse.

Q What role does Cecily's wealth play in Algernon's attitude to her?

Key vocabulary

Perrier-Jouet, Brut, '89: Perrier-Jouet is a brand of (very expensive) champagne. 'Brut' indicates the style (dry) and '89 (i.e. 1889) the year of vintage.

Scene 14 (pp.352–8)

Summary: *Lady Bracknell calls for Miss Prism; the governess discloses her shameful secret; Jack's family and name are revealed; the couples are united.*

The final scene proceeds – in stock melodrama fashion – as a series of revelations. The first of these concerns Miss Prism's identity as a former domestic servant in the home of Lady Bracknell's sister. As Lady Bracknell interrogates Miss Prism it becomes apparent that the latter harbours a dark secret. Her language resembles that of melodrama. She feels 'shame' for the incident that is 'for ever branded on [her] memory' and 'for which [she] can never forgive [her]self' (p.354).

As she recounts this story, a stage direction tells us Jack has '*been listening attentively*' (p.354). He leaves the stage momentarily and returns with the handbag, prompting the 'recognition scene'. Recognition scenes have a long history in English drama and often featured in melodrama in particular. One example is the scene at the end of Shakespeare's *Twelfth Night* where the twins Viola and Sebastian, who each thought the other dead, are reunited. They examine each other's face and body, searching for physical evidence before daring to believe in the other's identity. In *The Importance of Being Earnest*, the lost body of such recognition scenes is replaced with a handbag. Miss Prism scrutinises the bag as she might a person: 'It seems to be mine. Yes, here is the injury it received through the upsetting of a Gower Street omnibus in younger and happier days' (p.355).

Following the recognition of the handbag, Jack behaves as if he is a character in a problem play. He presumes Miss Prism's secret is the same as that of the typical problem play – that she has had a sexual relationship outside marriage and is thus a 'fallen woman'. In the problem play, the hero might have a speech critiquing the Victorian sexual double standard. This held that a woman who had a sexual transgression was 'ruined' and made an outcast, even if she expressed remorse, but the reputation of a man who transgressed was not sullied in the same way. Jack's speech to Miss Prism is a direct parody of the sentiments expressed in such plays. Under the impression that Miss Prism is his unmarried mother, he asks, 'Cannot repentance wipe out an act of folly? Why should there be one law for men, and another for women? Mother, I forgive you' (p.355). However, what Miss Prism seeks forgiveness for is not Jack's supposedly illegitimate birth, but her absorption in her three-volume novel, to the extent that she left him in a handbag at Victoria station.

Key point

That Jack's disappearance results from Miss Prism's preoccupation with a work of fiction alerts us to the importance of the written word in this play. What other examples of the importance of the written word can you identify? What is their influence? What do you think the play suggests about putting things in writing?

Miss Prism recoils in horror at Jack's suggestion that she is his unmarried mother, and informs him that Lady Bracknell holds the key to his identity. Lady Bracknell is able to tell him that he is the son of her sister Mrs Moncrieff and late brother-in-law General Moncrieff, and he is thus Algernon's older brother. Through this revelation Lady Bracknell fulfils the task she set Jack in Scene 4 – she has found him some relations. Yet the question of his name remains a mystery. Lady Bracknell knows Jack was named after his father but neither she nor Algernon can remember the General's first name. This is ironic considering the value she has placed on 'name' throughout the play. Farcically, the key to the mystery is on Jack's own bookshelf, in the Army Lists recording the names and ranks of officers. Jack leafs through the book to learn that the General's name was 'Ernest John', a discovery that represents a moment of triumph for Jack: 'I always told you, Gwendolen, my name was Ernest, didn't I? Well, it is Ernest after all. I mean it naturally is Ernest' (p.357).

The play closes with a 'tableau', a stage direction which requires the actors to hold a static pose for a moment before the curtain is lowered. The pose here emphasises the union of the three couples, with the actors standing in romantic attitudes.

Q What do you think Lady Bracknell's attitude would be during the tableau?

Key vocabulary

Temperance beverage: a non-alcoholic drink.

CHARACTERS & RELATIONSHIPS

Lady Bracknell

Key quotes

'I do not approve of anything that tampers with natural ignorance. Ignorance is like a delicate exotic fruit; touch it and the bloom is gone.' (p.309)

'To be born, or at any rate bred, in a hand-bag, whether it had handles or not, seems to me to display a contempt for the ordinary decencies of family life that reminds one of the worst excesses of the French Revolution.' (p.311)

'[She] is perfectly unbearable. Never met such a Gorgon.' (Jack, p.312)

Lady Bracknell is a formidable figure. She holds the most power in the play, being able to control all the characters and their hopes and desires with a single word (look, for example, at Miss Prism's reaction to Lady Bracknell's sudden appearance in Scene 14). It may seem odd to a contemporary reader for Lady Bracknell to hold so much power when we know that Victorian women were supposed to be submissive and self-effacing. Yet Victorian women did hold considerable power in certain arenas, such as Society. In Society circles, older women such as Lady Bracknell were not just arbiters of morality but also of fashion and etiquette. As members of the middle classes attempted to enter the ranks of Society, the rules of etiquette were strictly enforced and the female leaders of Society set the standards against which prospective participants were judged.

Lady Bracknell is an enforcer of etiquette par excellence; she is acutely conscious of social nuances. Her knowledge is shown at its extreme in the play, as she discusses features such as the most fashionable placement of the chin, or the social standing of individual houses: she denounces 149 Belgrave Square as being on the 'unfashionable side' (p.310). Although her focus on particulars is exaggerated for comic effect, it is nevertheless suggestive of the social policing that occurred in Victorian England. It also furthers the notion that style and social significance are mostly matters of appearance.

Lady Bracknell's viewpoint is not significantly challenged over the course of the play. Although Gwendolen disobeys her and Jack attempts to manipulate her through Cecily, she is not forced to succumb to their demands. Instead, circumstances change to allow her philosophy to remain triumphant. 'The doctors found out that Bunbury could not live', Algernon tells his aunt, 'so Bunbury died' (p.347), and the problem of Bunbury was solved. Similarly, Lady Bracknell decides Jack must find some relations, so Jack conveniently finds some relations.

John Worthing, J.P.

Key quotes

'When one is placed in the position of guardian, one has to adopt a very high moral tone on all subjects. It's one's duty to do so.' (p.301)

'For me you have always had an irresistible fascination. Even before I met you I was far from indifferent to you.' (Gwendolen, p.306)

'The fact is, Lady Bracknell, I said I had lost my parents. It would be nearer the truth to say that my parents seem to have lost me ... I don't actually know who I am by birth. I was ... well, I was found.' (p.310)

'I could deny it if I liked. I could deny anything if I liked.' (p.339)

Jack is the central figure of the play. His creation of Ernest, his courting of Gwendolen and the mystery of his origins are the key issues in the narrative. Jack constructs his country self as a man of duty and respectability. Not only is he Cecily's guardian but he is also the squire of a country estate and a Justice of the Peace (a local magistrate).

Like Algernon, Jack is leading a double life; however, we suspect he does so with less flair. His city self is also relatively more sombre, cautious and reserved than his flamboyant friend. Although he is the central figure, Jack is arguably a less memorable character than Algernon. He is frequently irritable and petulant, although he is also loyal and passionate. There is something rather childish about Jack: 'I don't see much fun in being christened along with *other* babies' (emphasis added, p.325) he tells Dr Chasuble. He seems to be in a state of arrested development.

Algernon Moncrieff

Key quotes

'I don't play accurately – anyone can play accurately – but I play with wonderful expression.' (p.295)

'If I am occasionally a little over-dressed, I make up for it by being always immensely over-educated.' (p.328)

'My duty as a gentleman has never interfered with my pleasures in the smallest degree.' (p.327)

Born into Society, Algernon presumably receives an income derived from his family's estates and investments. He lives the life of a leisured bachelor about town and indulges his taste for the finer things in life. His apartment is *'luxuriously and artistically furnished'* (p.295), and his chief preoccupations are eating and entertainment. With his commitment to beauty in interior decoration and personal dress, and his determination to treat life as 'art', Algernon is the most obvious representative of the Aesthetic movement in the play. He is not extravagantly wealthy, however, and there is the suggestion he lives beyond his means. When handed some letters in Scene 5 a stage direction notes that *'it is to be surmised that they are bills, as Algernon, after looking at the envelopes, tears them up'* (p.315). As Lady Bracknell says of Algernon, 'He has nothing, but he looks everything' (p.350).

Victorian audiences would have recognised Algernon as a 'dandy'. A dandy was a man who manipulated the rules of morality and etiquette to further his own interests. The dandy was preoccupied with style and fashion, and used wit as a weapon. With his charm, cleverness and sense of style, Algernon is the epitome (perfect example) of the dandy, as was Wilde himself.

Algernon is also not able to completely avoid the demands of the real world, in particular the demands of Society. In order to maximise his opportunities for pleasure he has created a fictional friend, the permanent invalid Bunbury. Algernon's claims of Bunbury's frequent ill-health enable him to escape unwelcome social engagements.

In Act Two, Algernon meets and falls in love with Cecily. He makes grand declarations of passion ('I have dared to love you wildly, passionately, devotedly, hopelessly', p.329), but is relatively unfazed by the complication of their engagement following Cecily's discovery of his true identity ('a perfectly wonderful Bunbury it is. The most wonderful Bunbury I have ever had in my life', p.340). He seems to be the same frivolous individual at the close of the play as he is at the beginning. However, he has also relinquished Bunbury ('Oh! I killed Bunbury this afternoon', p.347) and become engaged. Is this a surprising development considering his earlier attitude to marriage? Are his days of leading a double life truly over?

Hon. Gwendolen Fairfax

Key quotes

'Dear me, you are smart!' ... 'I am always smart! Am I not, Mr Worthing?' (Algernon and Gwendolen, p.303)

'What wonderfully blue eyes you have, Ernest! They are quite, quite blue. I hope you will always look at me just like that, especially when there are other people present.' (p.307)

'I never travel without my diary. One should always have something sensational to read in the train.' (p.336)

'I am known for the gentleness of my disposition, and the extraordinary sweetness of my nature, but I warn you, Miss Cardew, you may go too far.' (p.338)

There is something very sharp and hard about Gwendolen Fairfax, from the precise syllables of her name to her attitude to life. Gwendolen claims she is known for her gentleness and sweetness. However, Algernon's description of her as a 'brilliant, clever, thoroughly experienced young lady' (p.341) seems more accurate.

Gwendolen has been subjected to her mother's 'system'. This system is absurd in some respects (it has rendered her 'extremely short-sighted', p.334) and typical in others. For example, Gwendolen attends the University Extension Scheme, a form of self-improvement that was considered very suitable for a girl of Gwendolen's class. Yet although she is described as 'intellectual' (p.316), she seems more interested in appearing 'smart' in the sense of fashionable than 'smart' in the sense of intelligent. An early version of the play emphasised her priorities in her explanation of why she attended the Extension Scheme: 'I never return from any one of those lectures without having been excessively admired' (Donohue and Berggren 1995, p.313). Gwendolen's attention to issues of fashion is demonstrated in the tea scene. Her awareness of markers of style – sugar, cake – shows she is very much her mother's daughter.

Although she intends 'to develop in many directions' (p.303), Gwendolen does not appear to have undergone significant growth by the end of the play. In Act One her professions of passion are moderated by self-interest: 'although ... I may marry someone else, and marry often', she says to Jack, 'nothing that [Lady Bracknell] can possibly do can alter my eternal devotion to you' (p.315). Similarly, as Jack departs to find the handbag in the final scene, she tells him: 'If you are not too long, I will wait here for you all my life' (p.354). She also remains firm on her attitude to his name (although this, amusingly, contradicts her previous declarations of 'eternal devotion'): 'I never change, except in my affections' (p.356).

Cecily Cardew

Key quotes

'Cecily is not a silly romantic girl, I am glad to say. She has got a capital appetite, goes long walks and pays no attention at all to her lessons.' (Jack, p.313)

'I keep a diary in order to enter the wonderful secrets of my life. If I didn't write them down, I should probably forget all about them.' (Cecily, p.318)

'Cecily is the sweetest, dearest, prettiest girl in the whole world.' (Algernon, p.349)

At first Cecily appears to be a recognised Victorian type – the ingenue. The ingenue is a sweet, innocent, trusting and virtuous damsel. She is caring and gentle. In common with the type, Cecily seems to be very concerned about the welfare of others. In Victorian society, women were held as moral arbiters (judges) and it was thought that their goodness could have a positive effect on the people around them. Part of Cecily's excitement at Ernest's alleged wickedness is perhaps the chance it offers for her to reform him. She tells Miss Prism, 'I wish Uncle Jack would allow that unfortunate young man, his brother, to come down here sometimes. We might have a good influence over him' (p.318).

Yet Cecily is a paradoxical creature. When Algernon finally offers her the opportunity to reform Ernest she rejects it: 'I'm afraid I've no time, this afternoon' (p.321). She also leads her own double life, creating a fantasy world that she records as fact in her diary and steadfastly avoiding things (such as her lessons) that do not accord with that world. She believes so fervently and absolutely in her fantasy that it must come true – and it does.

Miss Prism

Key quotes

'I am not in favour of this modern mania for turning bad people into good people at a moment's notice. As a man sows so let him reap.' (p.318)

'The good ended happily, and the bad unhappily. That is what Fiction means.' (p.318)

'Maturity can always be depended on. Ripeness can be trusted. Young women are green.' (p.323)

The governess was a standard figure in Victorian literature. In accordance with the stereotype, Miss Prism is a mature spinster committed to learning and devoted to her work. The governess was often a member of the upper middle class whose financial difficulties had led her to use her good education in a life of domestic service. Scene 6 suggests Miss Prism's innate middle-class respectability. She appears to be the archetypal Victorian spinster governess, expressing values of duty, responsibility and self-improvement. This insight into her character sets up later opportunities for building comedy, such as the suggestion that she is a 'fallen woman'. Yet, the fact that she is very easily lured away from her duties to take a walk with Dr Chasuble is an early clue that perhaps she is not all that she seems.

Wilde plays with the governess stereotype by giving Miss Prism a secret life: she harbours a hidden passion for Dr Chasuble, has written a three-volume novel of 'more than usually revolting sentimentality' (p.354) and holds the key to the mystery of Jack's origins. Like Cecily, Miss Prism is paradoxical. The tensions in her character are reflected in her language, which is a bizarre combination of biblical quotations, Victorian maxims and sexual innuendo.

Like other governesses in Victorian literature, notably Charlotte Brontë's Jane Eyre, Miss Prism is rescued from a life of domestic servitude at the end of the play. Dr Chasuble finally professes his passion in Scene 14, a profession that will no doubt lead to marriage.

Rev. Canon Chasuble, D.D.

Key quotes

'And you do not seem to realize, dear Doctor, that by persistently remaining single, a man converts himself into a permanent public temptation.' (Miss Prism, p.322)

'Dr Chasuble is a most learned man. He has never written a single book, so you can imagine how much he knows.' (Cecily, p.332)

Dr Chasuble is a functional character in that his presence allows Jack and Algernon to further their re-christening plans. He also acts as a double to Miss Prism and comedy is built around their relationship, which in true farcical fashion is confirmed with declarations of passion at the close of the play. Yet Dr Chasuble is also a comic character in his own right – a version of the bumbling, ineffective older man (wedded to an institution such as education or religion and out of touch with the real world) who often appears in Victorian comedy. Wilde's satire of religion is introduced in Jack and Algernon's attitudes to the sacrament of baptism, and is further developed by Dr Chasuble's own comments on religious forms and functions. He appears preoccupied with the more obscure and specialised areas of theology, and much is made of his status as an intellectual. Yet he is not very effective – his sermons remain unpublished (a fact that links him to Miss Prism and her own unpublished writings).

Q What other connections can you identify between Miss Prism and Dr Chasuble? (You might look, for example, at their status as representatives of the great Victorian institutions of education and religion, or at their use of language.)

Lane

Key quotes

'Did you hear what I was playing, Lane?' ... 'I didn't think it polite to listen, sir.' (Algernon and Lane, p.295)

'I have only been married once. That was in consequence of a misunderstanding between myself and a young person.' (pp.295–6)

'Lane, you're a perfect pessimist.' ... 'I do my best to give satisfaction, sir.' (Algernon and Lane, p.316)

Although he appears only briefly in Act One and has few lines, quite a bit is conveyed about Lane's character. He is the model of the perfect butler in his grave manner, swift appearances and ability to obey orders. He also anticipates his master's needs, as witnessed in his support of Algernon's lie to Lady Bracknell about the cucumbers (p.304). There are suggestions that, like his master, Lane is himself leading a double life. He has had a mysterious early marriage and Algernon subtly accuses him of drinking his champagne, a suggestion the butler does not refute. These hints of passion and appetite contrast ironically with his very proper demeanour.

Merriman

Merriman appears frequently in Act Two and once in Act Three. He oversees the arrival of visitors to the house and serves tea to Gwendolen and Cecily in Scene 10 (where he is attended by an unnamed footman). Although Merriman conveys little humour in his dialogue there is scope for physical comedy in his frequent appearances and his responses to being ordered in and out. In Anthony Asquith's 1952 film of the play, Merriman is made the subject of a series of reaction shots in the tea scene, enhancing the sense of tension between Gwendolen and Cecily.

THEMES, IDEAS & VALUES

In both its own time and more recent times, critics and other readers have accused *The Importance of Being Earnest* of being about nothing. Yet it actually offers significant commentary on the values and mores of the society it represents.

Earnestness and triviality

Key quotes

'You look as if your name was Ernest. You are the most earnest-looking person I ever saw in my life.' (Algernon to Jack, p.300)

'Well, one must be serious about something, if one wants to have any amusement in life. I happen to be serious about Bunburying. What on earth you are serious about I haven't got the remotest idea. About everything, I should fancy. You have such an absolutely trivial nature.' (Algernon, p.340)

'My nephew, you seem to be displaying signs of triviality.' ... 'On the contrary, Aunt Augusta, I've now realized for the first time in my life the vital Importance of Being Earnest.' (Lady Bracknell and Jack, p.358)

Earnestness was a key concept in nineteenth-century England. Indeed the Victorian age 'appeared to value earnestness above all other virtues save belief in God' (Donohue and Berggren 1995, p.119). The quality of earnestness was associated with seriousness, sincerity, zeal and eagerness. It was also linked to the notion of 'duty'. In 1871 Samuel Smiles, a writer whose work articulated Victorian values, extolled duty as a force that 'embraces man's whole existence ... duty rounds the whole of life, from our entrance into it until our exit from it ... The abiding sense of duty is the very crown of character' (Donohue and Berggren 1995, p.203).

In practice, earnestness could mean priggishness, hypocrisy and humourlessness. Jack claims that as a guardian he is required 'to adopt a very high moral tone on all subjects'. It is his 'duty to do so' (p.301). The phrase 'high moral tone' and word 'duty' are synonyms for earnestness. However, rather than promoting earnestness as a good Victorian gentleman should, Jack figures it as a limiting and daunting force: 'a high moral tone can hardly be said to conduce very much to either one's health or one's happiness' (p.301). Jack's situation and his use of the word 'adopt' suggest that Wilde is exposing earnestness in Victorian society as a kind of pose or performance. The importance of correct appearances, rather than real feeling and genuine expression, is repeatedly satirised in the play. The fiction of being 'Ernest' rescues Jack from being 'earnest'.

Gwendolen and Cecily's insistence on marrying a man named Ernest ridicules Victorian priorities. Marriage to an earnest young man was a highly suitable desire for a Victorian girl. However, Gwendolen and Cecily are less concerned with whether their suitors are actually 'earnest' than with their being called 'Ernest'. This point is confirmed in their delight at the men's plans to be re-christened. Although Jack and Algernon's true names have been revealed, their willingness to become Ernest is enough for their fiancées. Again, this situation satirises the Victorian emphasis on surfaces: *appearing* to hold a virtue such as earnestness was more important than truly embodying it.

Triviality is opposed to earnestness. To be trivial is to be insignificant and lacking in seriousness; to treat something trivially is to treat it lightly and without the respect it is customarily afforded. Characters in the play repeatedly devote more time and energy to seemingly trivial concerns than they do to apparently more serious issues. Cecily is more preoccupied with the elaborate fiction she develops in her diary than she is with her lessons on geology or political economy. The state of the world is a far less interesting topic than the state of her mind. Miss Prism and Dr Chasuble spend more time socialising than they do attending to their respective occupations. Meanwhile, Jack and Algernon's lives in London appear to be conducted around a series of trivial pursuits: restaurants, the theatre, the club and the music-hall (p.314).

However, Wilde's play seems to celebrate rather than critique commitment to the trivial. In an interview before opening night, Wilde announced the play's philosophy: 'That we should treat all the trivial things of life very seriously, and all the serious things of life with sincere and studied triviality' (Beckson 1998, p.154). We can interpret this to suggest it is better to respond with intensity and passion to the things we desire and enjoy than it is to pay lip-service to worthy causes we are not really committed to. Ultimately the play suggests that it is better to be earnestly trivial (and thus true to oneself) than trivially earnest (and thus hypocritical).

In a letter written just a few months before Wilde began composing the play he claimed, 'seriousness of manner is the disguise of the fool' while 'triviality and indifference and lack of care is the robe of the wise man' (Donohue and Berggren 1995, p.292). Here Wilde also frames triviality as a kind of armour to shield oneself against the vulgarity and hypocrisy of the age.

Q Wilde subtitled the play 'A Trivial Comedy for Serious People' (p.291). What do you think he meant by this?

Truth and honesty

Key quotes

'The truth is rarely pure and never simple.' (Algernon, p.301)

'My dear fellow, the truth isn't quite the sort of thing one tells to a nice, sweet, refined girl.' (Jack, p.313)

'Gwendolen – Cecily – it is very painful for me to be forced to speak the truth. It is the first time in my life that I have ever been reduced to such a painful position, and I am really quite inexperienced in doing anything of the kind.' (Jack, p.339)

'Gwendolen, it is a terrible thing for a man to find out suddenly that all his life he has been speaking nothing but the truth.' (Jack, p.357)

As the play inverts the concepts of earnestness and triviality, so it inverts the values of truth and deception. Most of the characters in the play are frequent and expert liars. The most obvious source of deception is Jack and Algernon's double lives, yet there are other prominent examples. Lady Bracknell routinely lies to her husband: 'I do not propose to undeceive him', she declares, of having lied about Gwendolen's whereabouts, and 'indeed I have never undeceived him on any question' (p.346).

Some other examples of manipulations of the truth include:

- Lady Harbury's hair turning 'gold from grief' (p.304)
- Lane's lies about the availability of cucumbers (p.304)
- Gwendolen's brother Gerald's habit of proposing for practice (p.307)
- Cecily's lie about Miss Prism's headache (p.319)
- Miss Prism's sudden development of a headache (p.319)
- Cecily and Lady Dumbleton lying about their age (p.351).

The play suggests lying is an artistic practice that shows style and flair. Yet the Victorian emphasis on honesty and earnestness also has more serious implications. Jack and Algernon's lifestyles are shown to actually be dependent on their lies; their behaviours can only be maintained through a series of necessary fictions. The emphasis on lying, reflected in the characters' frequent manipulation of the truth, exposes the hypocrisy of the Victorian age. It is only through lying that the men can be true to themselves. This is a provocative and poignant message from a playwright who was himself forced to lead a double life in order to realise his desires.

Class and Society

Key quotes

'Really, if the lower orders don't set us a good example, what on earth is the use of them? They seem, as a class, to have absolutely no sense of moral responsibility.' (Algernon, p.296)

'Markby, Markby and Markby? A firm of the very highest position in their profession. Indeed I am told that one of the Mr Markby's is occasionally to be seen at dinner parties.' (Lady Bracknell, p.348)

'Never speak disrespectfully of Society, Algernon. Only people who can't get into it do that.' (Lady Bracknell, p.349)

The above quotes represent attitudes to the three broad classes of Victorian society. Algernon's use of inversion exposes his own class consciousness and the moral superiority of the 'upper orders'. Lady

Bracknell's comment about the appearance of Mr Markby reflects the growing mobility of the middle class. This solicitor is of such good standing that he has been accepted into upper-class dinner parties, events that were normally reserved for the elite. Her advice to Algernon demonstrates Society's desire to be seen as an exclusive enclave: a desire that perhaps intensified as individuals such as Mr Markby began to infiltrate its ranks.

As these comments indicate, the class system is a frequent target in *The Importance of Being Earnest,* particularly in terms of upper-class attitudes to those outside their class. For a deeper understanding of the function of class in the text, look also at Lane and Merriman's dialogue and demeanour, Miss Prism's description of her life in the Moncrieff household (pp.354–5) and Lady Bracknell's attitude to Gwendolen's maid (p.346).

Upper-class behaviour was governed by strict codes – the inhabitants of this world demanded precise and proper behaviour from each other. Rules set out in etiquette manuals governed dress, meals, housing, travel and social interaction. This regulation of behaviour is parodied in *The Importance of Being Earnest,* particularly through the characters of Lady Bracknell and Gwendolen. As the latter tells Cecily, 'sugar is not fashionable any more' and 'cake is rarely seen at the best houses nowadays' (p.337).

Lady Bracknell's comments at times reveal her anxiety about the permeability of class boundaries. For example, she claims that if education were more effective 'it would prove a serious danger to the upper classes, and probably lead to acts of violence in Grosvenor Square' (p.309). This kind of anxiety about class boundaries motivates her attitude to Jack's parentage – he must prove himself to be 'one of them'. By making Jack a member of the Moncrieff family the play fulfils this requirement with a vengeance. But, in doing so, what does it suggest about class distinctions?

Lady Bracknell makes frequent reference to unseen individuals, notably her husband Lord Bracknell, but also to other members of her social circle ('Lady Harbury', p.303; 'Mary Farquhar', p.304; the 'Duchess of Bolton', p.308; 'Lady Lancing', p.349; 'Lady Dumbleton', p.351). Lady Bracknell's references to other people emphasise the force and scale of Society. Society was a type of club, with entry based on family connections. As a consequence its members placed significant emphasis on parentage and there were strict protocols around marriage arrangements. This emphasis is reflected in Wilde's play.

Parentage

Key quotes

'Who was your father? He was evidently a man of some wealth. Was he born in what the Radical papers call the purple of commerce, or did he rise from the ranks of the aristocracy?' (Lady Bracknell, p.310)

'I would strongly advise you, Mr Worthing, to try and acquire some relations as soon as possible, and to make a definite effort to produce at any rate one parent, of either sex, before the season is quite over.' (Lady Bracknell, p.311)

'Every luxury that money could buy, including christening, had been lavished on you by your fond and doting parents.' (Lady Bracknell, p.356)

In Scene 4, Lady Bracknell identifies the two possible backgrounds she is prepared to contemplate for a prospective son-in-law. The first is that Jack's family has made their fortune in business, an option that was increasingly socially acceptable in the wake of the Industrial Revolution and the rise of capitalism. The second is that Jack's family, like that of her husband, belongs to the aristocracy and thus the upper orders of society.

Of course, Jack does not know his family background, a fact that horrifies Lady Bracknell. She interprets his 'carelessness' (p.310) in losing his parents as disrespect for lineage. In turn, she associates this disrespect with total class annihilation: 'To be born, or at any rate bred, in a hand-bag ... seems to me to display a contempt for the ordinary decencies of family life that reminds one of the worst excesses of the French Revolution' (p.311).

Lady Bracknell refuses to have the dignity and reputation of her own family name associated with an individual whose only family connection is a handbag. 'You can hardly imagine', she tells Jack, 'that I and Lord Bracknell would dream of allowing our only daughter – a girl brought up with the utmost care – to marry into a cloak-room, and form an alliance with a parcel' (p.311). The absurdity of the situation exposes the skewed values of Victorian society. Jack's name and lineage are of greater consequence than his character or love for Gwendolen. Lady Bracknell suggests his only hope is to 'try and acquire some relations as soon as possible' (p.311).

Christening can be seen as a symbol of Victorian anxieties about parentage and lineage. Family connections were the primary factor in an individual's class status, and the key means by which they could claim entry into Society. The sacrament of christening was thus also an important social ritual that bestowed a name, and all that the name represented, on an infant. It was a ritual that declared and confirmed the social status of an individual.

Marriage

Key quotes

'It is very romantic to be in love. But there is nothing romantic about a definite proposal. Why, one may be accepted. One usually is, I believe. Then the excitement is all over. The very essence of romance is uncertainty. If ever I get married, I'll certainly try to forget the fact.' (Algernon, p.297)

'An engagement should come on a young girl as a surprise, pleasant or unpleasant, as the case may be. It is hardly a matter that she could be allowed to arrange for herself.' (Lady Bracknell, p.308)

'No married man is ever attractive except to his wife.' (Miss Prism, p.322)

'Your brother was, I believe, unmarried, was he not?' ... 'Oh, yes.' ... 'People who live entirely for pleasure usually are.' (Dr Chasuble, Jack and Miss Prism, p.324)

The institution of marriage received significant attention in the nineteenth century. It underwent several reforms, including the creation of the Divorce Court in 1857 (an institution referred to by Jack in Scene 2). As a consequence the state of modern marriage was scrutinised everywhere, from the popular press to the pulpit. It became a frequent subject for representation in high literature, popular fiction and drama.

Key questions included the nature and indications of a 'good' marriage, and the possibility for female autonomy (independence) within marriage.

Marriage motivates the plot of Wilde's play and this is indicative of its importance in Victorian society. It held even more significance in the rarefied world of Society, which revolved around the marriage market. The highpoint of the season was the presentation of debutantes at court: an event indicating that these young women were now available as brides. In Society's understanding, marriage remained an economic and social partnership that must be carefully arranged to enhance the status of each party and their families. Algernon reflects this perspective when he hears of Jack's plans to propose to Gwendolen: 'I thought you had come up for pleasure? ... I call that business' (p.297). Lady Bracknell's business-like attitude to marriage is indicated when she takes out her 'list of eligible young men' in her interview with Jack (p.308). This list suggests she is continually doing research and consulting with trusted advisers such as 'the dear Duchess of Bolton' (p.308).

Wilde's play expresses some tension between traditional and progressive attitudes to marriage. Lady Bracknell suggests Gwendolen is acting improperly when she arranges her own engagement without parental interference: 'Pardon me, you are not engaged to anyone. When you do become engaged to someone, I, or your father, should his health permit him, will inform you of the fact' (p.308). Gwendolen is actually acting quite properly; at this time it was customary for the woman to decide for herself whether to accept a proposal or not. Gwendolen represents the modern, feminist viewpoint that a woman should be allowed to decide for herself. Lady Bracknell holds the more traditional, conservative understanding of marriage as an alliance to be carefully engineered.

One of the most interesting aspects of marriage in Wilde's text is Algernon's change of attitude to the subject. In Scene 2 he is cynical about marriage: 'You don't seem to realize, that in married life three is company and two is none' (p.302). Yet within moments of meeting Cecily he is proposing to her: 'I don't care for anybody in the whole world but you. I love you, Cecily. You will marry me, won't you?' (p.330).

Q How do you account for Algernon's extraordinary change of heart? Was his cynical attitude in Act One simply a performance? Is there something about Cecily that makes her his perfect match and thus capable of prompting such a change?

Q The play ends with six of the characters neatly paired off. The assumption is that Jack and Gwendolen; Algernon and Cecily; and Dr Chasuble and Miss Prism will be married. How do you respond to this ending? What do you think will be the distinctive qualities of each couple's marriage?

Nature and the 'natural'

Key quotes

'You have a town house, I hope? A girl with a simple, unspoiled nature, like Gwendolen, could hardly be expected to reside in the country.' (Lady Bracknell, p.309)

'Personally I cannot understand how anybody manages to exist in the country, if anybody who is anybody does.' (Gwendolen, p.337)

'I hope your hair curls naturally, does it?' ... 'Yes, darling, with a little help from others.' (Cecily and Algernon, p.331)

'Pretty child! your dress is sadly simple, and your hair seems almost as Nature might have left it. But we can soon alter all that.' (Lady Bracknell, p.349)

The Importance of Being Earnest plays with the division between the city and the country, which had a long tradition in English literature when Wilde wrote his play. This tradition presented the country as wholesome and unspoilt, and the city as wicked and corrupt. This standard classification is established in Act One when Jack describes his country self as a moral guardian and his city self as a pleasure seeker. Yet this dichotomy is then repeatedly challenged. Lady Bracknell tells Jack that a 'girl with a simple, unspoiled nature, like Gwendolen, could hardly be expected to reside in the country' (p.309). Meanwhile, the country characters are no less knowledgeable than their city counterparts, as evidenced by the passionate language of Cecily's journal and the double entendres of Miss Prism and Dr Chasuble's conversation.

Just as the characters criticise the country, so they also express suspicion and disdain for 'nature'. An item in its natural state has been sheltered from human intervention. From an Aesthetic or Decadent perspective it is thus less stylish or artistic than an item that has been manipulated by a man or woman. In 'Phrases and Philosophies for the Use of the Young', Wilde declared: 'The first duty in life is to be as artificial as possible. What the second duty is no one has as yet discovered' (Beckson 1998, p.263). In Act One, Algernon clearly upholds this philosophy. He is thoroughly committed to the pursuit of artificiality and demonstrates little interest in uncovering any other duties of life.

The play's valuing of artifice over nature is linked to its celebration of deception over truth. Artificially curled hair is, like the lie, a kind of artistic practice, a statement of style. And as Gwendolen reminds us, 'style, not sincerity, is the vital thing' (p.345).

From the observations regarding Lady Harbury's hair to those about Cecily's chin, the play repeatedly shows how the people in this world shy away from the natural. In addition, behaviours that are generally regarded as 'natural' and 'spontaneous', such as a marriage proposal, are portrayed as acts or performances. Gwendolen carefully orchestrates Jack's request for her hand in marriage, and prompts him to start over when he doesn't stick to the script. This can be seen in the minor characters' behaviours also: Lane's professional self can be read as a performance that he adapts according to the whims of his master.

Victorian institutions: religion and education

Key quotes

'The whole theory of modern education is radically unsound. Fortunately in England, at any rate, education produces no effect whatsoever. If it did, it would prove a serious danger to the upper classes, and probably lead to acts of violence in Grosvenor Square.' (Lady Bracknell, p.309)

'Every luxury that money could buy, including christening, had been lavished on you by your fond and doting parents.' (Lady Bracknell, p.356)

While there is no attempt at 'realism', *The Importance of Being Earnest* does make reference to the 'real world'. In doing so, it parodies cherished institutions such as religion and education: institutions that have been described as the 'twin pillars' of 'Victorian family life' (Raby 1988, p.121). Dr Chasuble arranges to have Jack and Algernon christened at fifteen-minute intervals and his 'sermon on the meaning of the manna in the wilderness can be adapted to almost any occasion' as he has 'preached it at harvest celebrations, christenings, confirmations, on days of humiliation and festal days' (p.324). These characters approach religious rituals as convenient commodities rather than serious spiritual sacraments.

Education was a key issue in nineteenth-century England. There was a particular focus on educational reform. Politicians and philanthropists worked to improve standards and make schooling more widely available, particularly for girls and working-class children. The push for reform was driven by an understanding of education as a civilising force that would strengthen an individual's morality as well as his or her intellect. This attitude also motivated the extension of educational and other self-improvement programs for adults of all classes. The University Extension Scheme attended by Gwendolen is an example of such a program. It was established to offer lectures to those unable or unwilling to attend university. Considering both Gwendolen and Cecily's attitudes to their education, the play seems to suggest that such programs were neither serious nor particularly effective.

As well as satirising the regard in which religion and education were held, Wilde's comedy also parodies the supposed respectability of these institutions. Their representatives – the spinster governess and the celibate cleric – are shown to harbour secret passions that are unleashed at the close of the play:

> Chasuble: [*to Miss Prism*]: Laetitia! [*Embraces her.*]
> Miss Prism: [*enthusiastically*]: Frederick! At last! (p.357)

In this exchange these characters sound more like the hero and heroine of a torrid melodrama than a dour parish priest and moralistic schoolmarm. At the last, the figureheads of education and religion are driven by the same passions and desires as everyone else in the play.

DIFFERENT INTERPRETATIONS

Different interpretations arise from different responses to a text. Over time, a text will give rise to a wide range of responses from its readers, who may come from various social or cultural groups and live in very different places and historical periods. Responses by critics and reviewers can be published in newspapers, journals and books, both online and in print. They can also be expressed in discussions among readers in the media, classrooms, book groups and so on. While there is no single correct reading or interpretation of a text, it is important to understand that an interpretation is more than a personal opinion – it is the justification of a point of view on the text. To present an interpretation of the text based on your point of view you must use a logical argument and support it with relevant evidence from the text.

Critical viewpoints

Critics of the first production generally found the play entertaining and extremely funny but lightweight and superficial. One critic described it as 'slight in structure and as devoid of purpose as a paper balloon', another like a 'mirage oasis in the desert, grateful and comforting to the weary eye – but when you come up close to it, behold! it is intangible, it eludes your grasp' (Beckson 1970, pp.189–90). Take some time to think about these comparisons. *How* is the play like a 'balloon' or a 'mirage'? Do you agree that it lacks substance beneath the shiny surface?

Following the first production, critic AB Walkeley attempted to explain why the play was so funny. He suggested laughter was provoked by 'the simultaneous recognition of the absurd and the natural' (Beckson 1970, p.198). He gives as an example Jack's entrance in mourning in Scene 7. That Jack is observing mourning for someone who is still alive (and actually in his house) is absurd, but considering the scope of his knowledge (his belief that he has absolute control over Ernest's activities) it is natural. Do you agree with Walkeley's theory? Can you identify other examples of this dynamic in the play? Walkeley's commentary also calls attention to the words 'absurd' and 'natural', both of which are uttered several times in the play. Note when the characters label something as either 'absurd' or 'natural'. Who uses these words and what value do they attach to them?

In the early twentieth century, as Wilde's works were collected and published and new productions mounted, *The Importance of Being Earnest* was increasingly seen by readers and audiences as his greatest play. Yet some critics denied its lasting value. Drama critic Eric Bentley noted the 'general conclusion has been that Wilde merely decorates a silly play with a flippant wit'. Bentley countered this view by claiming that the play's superb and original satire represented 'a new sort of comedy'. In Bentley's estimation the cleverness of the play derives from the fact that the issues being satirised receive repeated 'poisoned pin pricks' from the dramatist rather than an all-out attack (Tydeman 1982, p.102). While a single joke about marriage might be dismissed offhand, several satirical comments punctuated throughout the play can produce a ripple effect, allowing a more sustained and serious critique.

Perhaps the key area of critical interest in Wilde's play since the later twentieth century has been the extent to which it expresses an awareness of homosexual identity. The play has often been read as a product of the Decadent movement and *fin-de-siècle* culture, particularly in relation to issues of gender and sexuality. This focus has led some critics to identify a homosexual subtext in Wilde's play. In this reading the words 'Ernest' and 'Bunbury' become codes for homosexual identity and behaviour (Bristow 1992, p.208). This reading is linked to the significance of the doppelganger or 'double' in late-Victorian literature and culture: the idea that a moral, law-abiding individual might have a darker, deviant other self. This notion was confirmed for many Victorians when Wilde was arrested and details of his 'other life' were published in newspapers and periodicals. This idea of the double is also evident in other *fin-de-siècle* texts, notably Robert Louis Stevenson's *The Strange Case of Dr Jekyll and Mr Hyde* and Wilde's own novel *The Picture of Dorian Gray*.

Productions

Although there was a lingering sense of scandal around Wilde's plays for the first decade of the twentieth century, in the years following World War I *The Importance of Being Earnest* was repeatedly revived. Actor Sir John Gielgud oversaw important new productions of the play in 1930 and 1939. The latter production featured Edith Evans as Lady Bracknell. Her performance received tremendous acclaim and every subsequent Lady Bracknell has had to negotiate the legacy of Evans' performance, in particular her rendition of the immortal words 'A hand-bag?' near the end of the first act. There is evidence that Evans' performance was informed by her awareness of class distinctions. Evans was born into a lower middle-class family but left school at fifteen for a job as a milliner's assistant, which brought her into contact with ladies of fashion. Sir John Gielgud remembered her reading the handbag scene for some guests at a party: 'After the laughter had died down Edith handed me the book and remarked gravely, "I know those sort of women. They ring the bell and tell you to put a lump of coal on the fire"' (Stokes 1996, p.174). Drawing on her class consciousness, 'Evans's Bracknell exuded a particular form of arrogance that made little distinction between people and things' (Stokes 1996, p.174).

Regenia Gagnier, an influential contemporary scholar, claims that most modern productions are unable to capture the original power of Wilde's play. She suggests the strength of the first production derived from it being a mirror of its upper-class audience, coaxing them to laugh at their own pretensions and vices. In Gagnier's view, modern audiences miss Wilde's satirical targets and thus the force of his comedy (Gagnier 1986, p.133).

Q Do you agree that modern audiences would fail to recognise the satire in the play? How might a director enhance the satirical force of the text?

Film versions

The play has been adapted several times for film and television. I will focus on the two most widely available film versions: the 1952 film directed by Anthony Asquith and the 2002 film directed by Oliver Parker.

The Importance of Being Earnest, 1952

Edith Evans recorded her landmark interpretation of Lady Bracknell for posterity in Anthony Asquith's film. She was joined by a cast of acclaimed stage actors, including Margaret Rutherford who had appeared onstage opposite Evans as Miss Prism.

Through its cast, Asquith's film is closely associated with a theatrical style of performance and he enhances this dynamic by placing the action within defined, stage-like sets, and by framing the film as a play-within-a-play. The film opens as patrons gather in a theatre and the stage curtain opens to reveal Jack in his bath. As the camera pans down under the proscenium arch in the theatre, we are transported into the world of the film.

Framing the whole narrative as a performance opens the film up to possibilities generally confined to the theatre. The actors make no attempt at screen naturalism. Instead they present the characters in a style of deliberate artificiality and exaggerated seriousness. This style allows the comedy of Wilde's play to emerge.

Stephen Bourne has suggested that, in its artificiality, Asquith's film articulates the alleged homosexual subtext of Wilde's play by presenting heterosexuality as a performance. Giving as an example Jack and Gwendolen's kissing 'pose' in the final shot, Bourne suggests the film 'ridicules heterosexual romantic fantasies while keeping the sugar coating that allows the bitter pill to be swallowed' (Bourne 2006, p.39).

The true value of Asquith's film resides in its capture of the deliberately serious, artificial mode of performance that so suits Wilde's play, as well as its preservation of the performances of Edith Evans and Margaret Rutherford. There is also a sense of authority and authenticity about this film as several members of the cast and crew had been born in the 1880s or earlier, and thus represented a physical connection with the original production and Wilde's world.

The Importance of Being Earnest, 2002

Oliver Parker's film takes a vastly different approach from the 1952 film, attempting a more naturalistic interpretation of the plot and characters. In Parker's film the action of the play has been significantly re-structured and scenes, locations and characters have been added. The point of the re-structuring appears to be making the action more coherent from a modern perspective, and sketching in the backgrounds of the characters. For example, Jack is shown leaving his estate in the clothes of a country squire and changing on the train to arrive in London in the attire of a cosmopolitan gentleman. Thus his double identity is suggested before he has even met Algernon.

Parker's film provides concrete images for several items and incidents that are only suggested in the play. Jack and Algernon's first meeting takes place amidst the chorus-girls, courtesans and gamblers that might have kept them company after their dinner at Willis's. Lady Bracknell's mention of her lack of money at the time of marrying Lord Bracknell is accompanied by a flashback presenting her earlier self as a chorus-girl who met her husband at the theatre. The flashback confirms the notion, that is merely implied in Wilde's text, of her as social-climber and outsider.

Important aspects of the original are re-interpreted in Parker's film. Whereas in the play Jack is more preoccupied with changing his name to Ernest than uncovering the truth of his identity, the film adds several scenes that show him researching the mystery of his origins. After Jack has consulted the Army Lists and declared that his name really is Ernest, Lady Bracknell examines the entry and the film cuts to the page she is reading. The name 'Moncrieff, John' is clearly shown. Her discovery prompts her line 'My nephew, you seem to be displaying signs of triviality' and Jack's response: 'On the contrary, Aunt Augusta, I've now realized for the first time in my life the vital Importance of Being Earnest' (p.358). This is a significant intervention into the original and alters the meaning of the play's final line, and thus of the entire play.

As a mainstream film from a leading studio (Miramax), and featuring a major star (Reese Witherspoon), the 2002 film is designed to appeal to a mass audience. In accordance with the dominant model of mainstream cinema, the actors adopt an understated, naturalistic style of performance. In attempting to present the characters naturalistically – to give them psychological motivations and make them dramatically interesting – the film demonstrates the importance of style to Wilde's text. The comedy is dependent on a style of heightened seriousness and artificiality. Presenting the text in a naturalistic mode divests it of some of its humour.

Two interpretations

Reading 1

Wilde's play demonstrates that reality is more important than fantasy.

According to this statement, the play suggests that people should focus on how things really are, rather than simply taking an amusing or even illusory view of their circumstances. In order to support this view of the text, you would need to analyse the function and value of the characters' perceptions and test them against their reality. When are the characters forced to relinquish their reliance on fiction? In what ways are they ultimately bound by the material facts of life?

A significant support to this argument is the fact that Jack and Algernon are required to abandon Ernest and Bunbury. In Act One each man testifies to the importance of their doubles in their lives, but by the end of the play they have been forced to relinquish them. They cannot continue into married life and therefore progress and grow as individuals while they are dependent on these fictions.

There are other, less obvious, pieces of evidence that support this argument. For example, as a younger woman Miss Prism occupied herself by writing a three-volume novel. This could be dismissed as a harmless pastime if not for the fact that her absorption in the fiction led to her loss of baby Jack. His entire life has been affected by her ill-timed focus on fantasy rather than reality.

Reading 2

Wilde's play suggests that the fictions we create are more valuable than the material realities of our lives.

In contrast to the first reading, this statement sees the play as placing more importance on the way we perceive life than on the material facts of our existence. Again, you need to analyse the function and value of the characters' perceptions and test them against their reality. This time, rather than looking at their fantasies as limiting or inadequate, examine how the characters' lives are enriched and expanded by the fictions they create.

Certain characters are more animated by fantasy than reality. Cecily is an obvious example. The stories that she devises and records in her diary have more real bearing on her life than the lessons in geology and German grammar that she takes with Miss Prism. Her diary stories influence her life in ways that her lessons do not. She is never required to draw on her knowledge of geology or political economy, but the fictions she has written enable her engagement to Algernon and may influence him to fall in love with her.

Perhaps the most striking example of the value and necessity of fiction in these characters' lives is Jack and Algernon's dependence on their imaginary doubles Ernest and Bunbury. These fictional counterparts enable them to be true to themselves in a way that reality does not allow.

QUESTIONS & ANSWERS

This section focuses on your own analytical writing on the text, and gives you strategies for producing high quality responses in your coursework and exam essays.

Essay writing – an overview

An essay is a formal and serious piece of writing that presents your point of view on the text, usually in response to a given essay topic. Your 'point of view' in an essay is your interpretation of the meaning of the text's language, structure, characters, situations and events, supported by detailed analysis of textual evidence.

Analyse – don't summarise

In your essays it is important to avoid simply summarising what happens in a text:

- A **summary** is a description or paraphrase (retelling in different words) of the characters and events. For example: 'Macbeth has a horrifying vision of a dagger dripping with blood before he goes to murder King Duncan'.
- An **analysis** is an explanation of the real meaning or significance that lies 'beneath' the text's words (and images, for a film). For example: 'Macbeth's vision of a bloody dagger shows how deeply uneasy he is about the violent act he is contemplating – as well as his sense that supernatural forces are impelling him to act'.

A limited amount of summary is sometimes necessary to let your reader know which part of the text you wish to discuss. However, always keep this to a minimum and follow it immediately with your analysis (explanation) of what this part of the text is really telling us.

Plan your essay

Carefully plan your essay so that you have a clear idea of what you are going to say. The plan ensures that your ideas flow logically, that your argument remains consistent and that you stay on the topic. An essay plan should be a list of **brief dot points** – no more than half a page. It includes:

- your central argument or main contention – a concise statement (usually in a single sentence) of your overall response to the topic. See 'Analysing a sample topic' for guidelines on how to formulate a main contention.
- three or four dot points for each paragraph indicating the main idea and evidence/examples from the text. Note that in your essay you will need to *expand* on these points and *analyse* the evidence.

Structure your essay

An essay is a complete, self-contained piece of writing. It has a clear beginning (the introduction), middle (several body paragraphs) and end (the last paragraph or conclusion). It must also have a central argument that runs throughout, linking each paragraph to form a coherent whole.

See examples of introductions and conclusions in the 'Analysing a sample topic' and 'Sample answer' sections.

The introduction establishes your overall response to the topic. It includes your main contention and outlines the main evidence you will refer to in the course of the essay. Write your introduction *after* you have done a plan and *before* you write the rest of the essay.

The body paragraphs argue your case – they present evidence from the text and explain how this evidence supports your argument. Each body paragraph needs:

- a strong **topic sentence** (usually the first sentence) that states the main point being made in the paragraph
- **evidence** from the text, including some brief quotations
- **analysis** of the textual evidence explaining its significance and explanation of how it supports your argument

- **links back to the topic** in one or more statements, usually towards the end of the paragraph.

Connect the body paragraphs so that your discussion flows smoothly. Use some linking words and phrases like 'similarly' and 'on the other hand', though don't start every paragraph like this. Another strategy is to use a significant word from the last sentence of one paragraph in the first sentence of the next.

Use key terms from the topic – or synonyms for them – throughout, so the relevance of your discussion to the topic is always clear.

The conclusion ties everything together and finishes the essay. It includes strong statements that emphasise your central argument and provide a clear response to the topic.

Avoid simply restating the points made earlier in the essay – this will end on a very flat note and imply that you have run out of ideas and vocabulary. The conclusion is meant to be a logical extension of what you have written, not just a repetition or summary of it. Writing an effective conclusion can be a challenge. Try using these tips:

- Start by linking back to the final sentence of the second-last paragraph – this helps your writing to 'flow', rather than just leaping back to your main contention straight away.
- Use synonyms and expressions with equivalent meanings to vary your vocabulary. This allows you to reinforce your line of argument without being repetitive.
- When planning your essay, think of one or two broad statements or observations about the text's wider meaning. These should be related to the topic and your overall argument. Keep them for the conclusion, since they will give you something 'new' to say but still follow logically from your discussion. The introduction will be focused on the topic, but the conclusion can present a wider view of the text.

Essay topics

1. 'Although Jack is the principal character, Algernon is really the hero of Wilde's play.' Do you agree?
2. 'Jack and Gwendolen, and Cecily and Algernon, make suitable partners for each other.' Do you agree?
3. 'Lady Bracknell is the most powerful figure in the play.' Discuss.
4. '*The Importance of Being Earnest* presents a scornful attitude towards learning and education.' Discuss.
5. Discuss the importance of names and naming in *The Importance of Being Earnest*.
6. 'In *The Importance of Being Earnest*, the characters talk about the importance of duty, but they act on desire.' Discuss.
7. Oscar Wilde said, "we should treat all the trivial things of life very seriously, and all the serious things of life with sincere and studied triviality". Is this the view presented by the play?
8. 'Wilde's play is a satire of Victorian values and institutions.' Discuss the play as a satire, focusing on at least one target in depth.
9. How does Wilde use language to develop character in the play? Focus on one or two characters in detail.
10. Discuss the use of pairing and mirroring – for example, of characters, incidents, items and language – in *The Importance of Being Earnest*.

Vocabulary for writing on *Earnest*

Dramatic irony: a dramatic technique whereby the reader or audience is aware of developments that have not yet been revealed to the characters. *The Importance of Being Earnest* depends on dramatic irony for much of its comedy. Examples include Jack's lack of awareness of Ernest's presence in his house at the start of Scene 7, and Gwendolen and Cecily's mistaken belief that they have become engaged to the same man in Scene 10.

Genre: refers to the classification of a text within one or more literary forms. *The Importance of Being Earnest* is related to several dramatic genres, including farce, melodrama and the problem play.

Lampoon: a broader, less subtle form of satire, in which the intention to ridicule is more obvious. *The Importance of Being Earnest* lampoons Victorian figures such as the Society matron.

Paradox: a statement that seems to contradict itself. Paradox as a comic technique makes us laugh because it is unexpected. It also invites us to re-examine the worth of the original proposition.

Parody: the mimicking of a style or form (for example a style of writing) for comic effect. Wilde's play parodies Victorian dramatic forms such as melodrama.

Satire: the use of comedy to ridicule folly, vice, pretension or fashion. Some of the targets of satire in the play include Victorian earnestness, the importance of family connections in Society and the fashion for self-improvement. Satire is closely related to ***parody*** and ***lampoon***.

Analysing a sample topic

'Lady Bracknell is the most powerful figure in the play.' Discuss.

This question asks you to consider the status of Lady Bracknell. Before formulating a response, start by brainstorming questions this topic provokes and jotting down answers. Such questions might include:

- *Is* Lady Bracknell powerful?
- If so, what is the nature of her power?
- Whom does she have power over?
- How does she wield her power?
- How does her power develop over the course of the play? Is it strengthened or challenged?

Your answers to these questions will help you develop an *opinion* and *main contention* on the topic.

Sample introduction

> Lady Bracknell is a formidable figure in *The Importance of Being Earnest*; her power derives from her status as a social and moral decision-maker. The other characters attempt to work against her strictures, but they are ultimately powerless in the face of her control.

Paragraph outline

Paragraph 1: Lady Bracknell's power over issues of morality, style and social significance.

- She subjects others to her standards of morality. For example, she invites Algernon to choose the music for her party but emphasises her continued control over the selection: 'I'm sure the programme will be delightful, after a few expurgations. French songs I cannot possibly allow' (p.305).
- She is able to dictate the terms of fashion. For example, she proclaims 149 Belgrave Square on the 'unfashionable side' but adds 'that could easily be altered' (p.310).

Paragraph 2: Lady Bracknell's power over other characters.

- She commands authority through her language and demeanour. Following their interview Jack describes her as a 'Gorgon' (p.312), a mythical creature who turned all who looked on her into stone. Lady Bracknell has a similar effect. Miss Prism '*grows pale and quails*' (p.353) at the mere sight of her in Scene 14.
- She allows her daughter little autonomy. When Gwendolen announces her engagement to Jack, Lady Bracknell replies: 'Pardon me, you are not engaged to anyone' (p.308).
- She exerts total control over Gwendolen's life and decisions. Her parenting 'system' has moulded Gwendolen's very body, leaving her 'extremely short-sighted' (p.334).
- Gwendolen herself admits she is powerless in the face of this tyrant: 'Whatever influence I ever had over mamma, I lost at the age of three' (pp.314–15).

Paragraph 3: Lady Bracknell's power over the plot.

- She is responsible for both the key dilemma of the play (Jack's need to find some relations) and its solution.
- Miss Prism says of Lady Bracknell to Jack: 'There is the lady who can tell you who you really are' (p.356).
- She is the only character without a double, enhancing her sense of power over the course of the action.

Sample conclusion

> Although the major characters attempt to determine the course of their lives they are ultimately bound by Lady Bracknell's philosophy of social significance. She regards name and family connections as the basis of social status, and social status as the most important aspect of identity.
>
> Lady Bracknell achieves her aim. In Act One she tells Jack to find some relations and by the end of Act Three he has. This has only occurred through her intervention. Her philosophy reigns triumphant at the end of the play.

An alternative argument

The above analysis assumes an agreement with the proposition. It is also possible to argue against the proposition, to show that Lady Bracknell is not as powerful as she initially appears. In order to support such an argument you might draw on the following evidence:

- Gwendolen escapes from her mother (twice!) to pursue her relationship with Jack.
- Algernon is able to manipulate his aunt's demands through the fiction of Bunbury.
- Jack is more eager to address Gwendolen's desire for him to be named Ernest than he is to fulfil Lady Bracknell's demand for him to find some relations.

SAMPLE ANSWER

Oscar Wilde said, "we should treat all the trivial things of life very seriously, and all the serious things of life with sincere and studied triviality". Is this the view presented by the play?

To describe something as 'trivial' is to suggest it is insignificant, insubstantial and lacks seriousness. To treat something 'trivially' is to treat it lightly, without the seriousness it should be accorded. Thus 'triviality' and 'seriousness' stand in opposition. In the Victorian era, triviality was frowned upon while seriousness was applauded. *The Importance of Being Earnest* presents a topsy-turvy version of the Victorian world in which the principal characters are frequently preoccupied with trivial concerns and trivialise seemingly more serious issues. Amidst the fun this fantasy creates, some deeper truths emerge.

In Act Three, Algernon criticises Jack for his misplaced seriousness: 'What on earth you are serious about I haven't got the remotest idea. About everything, I should fancy. You have such an absolutely trivial nature'. Algernon implies that Jack, by acting as if he is serious about many things, ends up valuing nothing and therefore trivialising everything. This hits at the heart of Victorian ideas about virtue and respectability. It was considered 'hypocrisy' to espouse virtue and act on desire. Wilde's play shows that desire is an important and necessary part of life. Algernon recognises this, and celebrates his desires for trivial things without pretending to be serious about matters that are of less importance to him. Similarly, Cecily treats the fiction of her romance with Ernest with more seriousness than she does her lessons. Wilde's play celebrates this approach as one that is conducive to both 'health' and 'happiness'.

Algernon is a master of the art of 'sincere and studied' triviality. He takes trivial concerns – such as food and fashion – intensely seriously. Algernon's attitude reflects principles of the Aesthetic movement. The Aesthetic movement encouraged the notion of 'art for art's sake', asking us to value things for their essence, for what they are, rather than for what they represent or for their social significance. Algernon reflects this perspective throughout the play but particularly in his attitude to eating. He delights in the wonder of freshly cut cucumber sandwiches and buttery toasted muffins. He treats these trivial items, seemingly lacking in real substance, with seriousness. For him, it would be shallow not to do this.

Wilde's play repeatedly shows characters treating trivial issues with undue gravity. Jack is more preoccupied with changing his name to Ernest than with uncovering the truth of his origins. Considering Lady Bracknell's attitude to lineage, it may seem that he is privileging a trivial concern over one that is more serious. However, at this point it is more important for Jack to maintain his relationship with Gwendolen, which requires him to be called Ernest, than it is to placate Lady Bracknell. His attitude is well judged, because even after his identity as a member of the Moncrieff family is established, Gwendolen remains firm on the point of his name. She *will not* marry him unless he is called Ernest. His priorities have been in the right place all along.

As the play invites us to give trivial issues serious consideration, so it trivialises institutions and concerns customarily treated with high seriousness. Religious rituals, such as Dr Chasuble's sermon on the manna in the wilderness, are key targets. The play presents the sermon as a multi-purpose religious cure for all human problems. By trivialising the sermon and its uses, Wilde is critiquing the treatment of religion as a shallow symbol or social ritual rather than a true spiritual sacrament. Similarly, Jack and Algernon treat the sacrament of baptism as a convenient means of changing one's name rather than as a significant religious ritual. Beneath the comedy, their trivial attitudes invite serious consideration of the function of christening, and in turn the emphasis on name and lineage, in Victorian society. By satirising Victorian issues and institutions such as religion, *The Importance of Being Earnest* does not deny the importance or power of these things but invites questions about our attitudes to them.

By treating trivial issues with seriousness and serious issues with triviality, *The Importance of Being Earnest* can be read as an invitation to reconsider our values and priorities. Its concern for the trivial encourages a playful attitude to life and recognition of the importance of desire. Its 'sincere and studied' trivialisation of serious issues forces our attention on their weaknesses and inconsistencies. By treating desire with seriousness and trivialising the pomposity and false earnestness of Victorian mores, the play asks us to consider the true values of humanity.

REFERENCES & READING

Text

Wilde, Oscar 2000, *The Importance of Being Earnest and Other Plays*, Penguin Classics, London.

Films

The Importance of Being Earnest 1952, dir. Anthony Asquith, British Film Makers. Starring Michael Redgrave, Michael Denison and Edith Evans.

The Importance of Being Earnest 2002, dir. Oliver Parker, Miramax Films. Starring Colin Firth, Rupert Everett and Judi Dench.

Other references

Abrams, MH (ed.) 1993, *The Norton Anthology of English Literature*, 6th edn, Norton, New York.

Beckson, Karl 1970, *Oscar Wilde: The Critical Heritage*, Routledge and Kegan Paul, London.

Beckson, Karl 1998, *The Oscar Wilde Encyclopedia*, AMS Press, New York.

Bourne, Stephen 2006, 'Behind the Masks: Anthony Asquith and Brian Desmond Hurst', in Robin Griffiths, ed., *British Queer Cinema*, Routledge, London, pp.35–46.

Bristow, Joseph 1992, 'Critical Commentary', in Oscar Wilde, *The Importance of Being Earnest and Other Writings*, Routledge, London, pp.202–31.

Donohue, Joseph and Berggren, Ruth 1995, *Oscar Wilde's The Importance of Being Earnest*, Colin Smythe, Buckinghamshire.

Gagnier, Regenia 1986, *Idylls of the Marketplace: Oscar Wilde and the Victorian Public*, Stanford University Press, Stanford.

Landow, George P 2003, *The Victorian Web*, Brown University, victorianweb.org

Raby, Peter 1988, *Oscar Wilde*, Cambridge University Press, Cambridge.

Stokes, John 1996, *Oscar Wilde: Myths, Miracles and Imitations*, Cambridge University Press, Cambridge.

Tydeman, William 1982, *Wilde: Comedies*, Macmillan, London.